AN ILLUSTRATED DATA GUIDE TO

BATTLE TANKS
OF WORLD WAR II

Compiled by
Christopher Chant

TIGER BOOKS INTERNATIONAL
LONDON

This edition published in 1997 by
Tiger Books International PLC
Twickenham

Published in Canada in 1997 by
Vanwell Publishing Limited
St. Catharines, Ontario

© Graham Beehag Books
Christchurch
Dorset

Printed in Hong Kong

ISBN 1-85501-856-X

CONTENTS

A22 Infantry Tank Mk IV Churchill

Specification: A22 Infantry Tank Mk IV Churchill III

Country of origin: UK

Type: Infantry tank

Crew: Five

Combat weight: 87,360lb (39,626kg)

Dimensions: Length overall 25ft 2in (7.67m); width 10ft 8in (3.25m); height overall 8ft 2in (2.49m)

Armament system: One 6pdr (57mm) QF Mk III L/43 or Mk V L/50 rifled gun with 84 rounds, two 7.92mm (0.312in) Besa machine-guns (one co-axial and one bow) with 9,450 rounds, one 0.303in (7.7mm) Bren AA machine-gun with 600 rounds, and one 2in (50.8mm) bomb thrower with 30 rounds; the turret was electrically operated, the main gun was stabilised in neither elevation (-12.5° to +20°) nor azimuth (360°), and simple optical sights were fitted

Armour: Bolted and welded steel varying in thickness between 0.63 and 4.1in (16 and 104mm)

Powerplant: One 350hp (261kW) Bedford Twin-six petrol engine with 150 Imp gal (682 litres) of fuel plus provision for 32.5 Imp gal (147.7 litres) of additional fuel in a jettisonable external tank

Performance: Speed, road 15.5mph (24.9km/h); range, road 120 miles (193km) with external fuel; fording 3ft 4in (1.01m) without preparation; gradient 58%; vertical obstacle 2ft 6in (0.76m); trench 10ft 0in (3.05m); ground clearance 20in (0.51m)

After the Valentine came the UK's most important infantry tank of World War II, the A22 Infantry Tank Mk IV Churchill. This vehicle was planned in 1939 as replacement for the Matilda II, the operational scenario envisaged by the War Office comprising a Western Front not dissimilar to that in

The Churchill was one of the most successful and important British-designed battle tanks of World War II, and is seen here in the form of a Churchill Armoured Recovery Vehicle Mk II with its large front jib erected for the recovery of a stranded or damaged tank.

France during World War I: this scenario called for a tank that was in essence a modern version of the rhomboidal tanks of that war, with thick armour, good but not exceptional armament, and the ability to move without undue difficulty in a heavily shelled area. In September 1939 the specification for an A20 infantry tank was issued, and design work was entrusted to Harland and Wolff in Belfast as part of the government's sensible but long overdue policy of diversifying tank design and construction capability. Harland and Wolff built four prototypes by June 1940, and these revealed a striking similarity to World War I practices, with a generally rhomboidal shape for good trench-crossing capability, and a main armament of two 2pdr (40mm) guns located in side sponsons. The type was also planned with a central turret, but in the event none of the prototypes was fitted with turret or armament.

In June 1940 the French campaign ended, and with it the War Office discarded its notions of latter-day trench warfare and thus the A20's *raison d'étre*. The design had good features in its hull and running gear, however, and these formed the basis of the vehicle designed by Dr H.E. Merritt, the director of tank design, when the revised A22 specification was released to Vauxhall Motors. The country's desperate situation after the defeat at Dunkirk was reflected in the War Office's stipulation that production of the A22 should begin within one year, even though it was realised that so rushed a programme would necessarily entail a number of inbuilt faults in the first model. Design began in July 1940 and the first A22 prototype appeared in December 1940, with the initial Churchill I production tanks coming off the line in June 1941 to inaugurate a programme that finally produced 5,640 Churchill tanks before production was completed in October 1945.

Results of tank development in the late 1930s, and the lessons of the Polish and Western campaigns waged and won by the Germans in 1939 and 1940, had resulted in a tank that was both lower and better protected than its predecessors: in the first Churchills the armour varied in thickness from a minimum of 0.63in (16mm) to a maximum of 4in (102mm). But two short-term limitations were the inadequate armament and the problem-prone engine. By 1940 it had been realised that the 2pdr (40mm) gun was too feeble a weapon for effective anti-tank employment, and lacked a significant HE shell capability: a considerably more effective weapon, the 6pdr (57mm) gun, was already in existence but not in production, and in the days after Dunkirk the decision was made to keep the obsolescent gun in large-scale production rather than phase in the 6pdr (57mm) weapon. So far as the Churchill was concerned, this meant that a substantial 86,240lb (39,118kg) vehicle was fitted with a turret carrying obsolescent armament. The situation was partially remedied in the Churchill I by the installation of a 3in (76.2mm) howitzer in the front plate of the hull: this howitzer had a useful support capability, although the installation can be regarded as poor because of the limited traverse imposed by the semi-recessed position of the front plate behind the projecting forward horns of the running gear. Compensating in part for the armament deficiency was the excellent ammunition stowage, amounting to one hundred and fifty 2pdr (40mm) rounds and fifty-eight 3in (76.2mm) rounds without hampering the volume left for the crew of five (driver and gunner in the nose compartment, and the commander, gunner and loader in the spacious turret).

The other major limitation was the engine, a custom-designed Bedford petrol unit that was essentially a pair of six-cylinder truck engines lying on their sides and married to a common crankcase. This petrol unit developed only 350hp (261kW), giving the Churchill a distinctly modest power-to-weight ratio, and was plagued with reliability problems in its first year of service. Unreliability was of course a disadvantage in itself, but it was exacerbated by the Churchill's poor engine installation. The War Office had demanded a readily accessible engine compartment, but this failed to materialise and even comparatively minor problems demanded the removal of the entire engine. Development and service experience gradually eliminated the engine problems, and this in turn reduced the adverse effect of the poor engine installation. Ultimately the Churchill became a notably reliable tank. The engine's power was transmitted to the rear drive sprockets by a flexible transmission system, and driving was both easier and more precise than on other British tanks of the period through the use of hydraulics in the clutch and steering systems. The latter was also the first operational use of the Merritt-Brown regenerative system, which was less tiring for the driver and allowed increasingly sharp turns with reducing speed, until in neutral the driver could turn the tank on its own length. The running gear was also good, given the obvious constraints of the tank's design for the infantry role. There were 11 small independent coil-sprung road wheels on each side: these made for a fairly bumpy ride, but were cheap to manufacture and install; the tank could survive the loss of several road wheels without loss of mobility, and could be repaired without difficulty in the field.

The Churchill remained in service with the British army from 1941 to 1952, and underwent considerable development, especially during World War II. In addition to the Churchill I, there was also a Churchill I CS with a second 3in (76.2mm) howitzer in the turret in place of the 2pdr (40mm) gun. The Churchill II was similar to the Churchill I in all but armament, where the hull-mounted howitzer was replaced by a 7.92mm (0.312in) Besa machine-gun to complement the co-axial weapon in the turret. These first two marks may be regarded as pilot models, and the A22 design began to reach maturity in the Churchill III, which was a much-improved 87,360lb (39,626kg) model that appeared in March 1942 with an all-welded turret accommodating the 6pdr (57mm) gun for greater anti-tank capability; the Mk III also introduced the large mudguards that were fitted on all later marks and retrofitted to the first two variants. The Churchill IV was similar to the Mk III except for its turret, which was a cast rather than welded unit; in North Africa some Mk IVs were revised to the so-called Churchill IV (NA 75) standard with the 75mm (2.95in) main gun and 0.3in (7.62mm) Browning co-axial machine-gun of the M3 Grant medium tank. The Churchill V was the first genuine close-support version of the series, and was armed with a 94mm (3.7in) Tank Howitzer Mk I, the same weapon as that installed in the Centaur IV. The final variant of the initial Churchill series was the Churchill VI, another gun tank and modelled on the Mk IV with the exception of the main armament, which was a 75mm (2.95in) Mk 5 weapon of the type installed on the Centaur III and on the Cromwell V, VI and VII.

The use of this weapon is an interesting commentary on the state of British tank gun development, for it compared unfavourably with the contemporary 75mm (2.95in) KwK 42 L/70 weapon used in the PzKpfw V Panther. The British Mk 5 weapon was 112.6in (2.86m) long and weighed 692lb (314kg), firing its 13.75lb (6.24kg) projectile with a muzzle velocity of 2,030ft (619m) per second; by comparison, the KwK 42 gun was 218in (5.54m) long and weighed 1,389lb (630kg), but fired its 15lb (6.8kg) projectile with a muzzle velocity of 3,068ft (935m) per second. The German gun was thus longer and heavier than the British weapon, but this translated into higher muzzle velocity with a larger projectile, producing an armour penetration of 3.62in (92mm) compared with only 2.68in (68mm) for the British gun.

The Churchill VI was essentially an interim variant pending deliveries of the considerably upgraded A22F (later A42) Infantry Tank Churchill VII. The origins of the variant reach back to the War Office's realisation that appliqué armour (additional thicknesses of plate attached over key areas) was not the optimum solution to the problem of improving protection. The A22F specification therefore called for a maximum armour thickness of 6in (152mm), although this was to be of the integral rather than appliqué type. The resultant Churchill VII retained the basic configuration and shape of the earlier marks, but was extensively revised to allow the incorporation of thicker armour in the structure, and also to incorporate the many features that had been shown to be desirable in earlier variants. The armour varied in thickness from a minimum of 0.98in (25mm) to a maximum of 6in (152mm), and this increased the tank's basic weight to 89,600lb (40,643kg). The engine remained unaltered, so the tank's maximum speed was reduced from 16 to 12.75mph (25.75 to 20.5km/h): this was a governed speed produced by a gearbox with lower ratios to avoid overtaxing the strengthened suspension. The main armament was the same 75mm (2.95in) gun as fitted in the Mk VI, with a single-baffle muzzle brake, but the turret was a composite unit with the horizontal roof welded to

The Churchill Crocodile was an armoured flamethrower with the flame gun replacing the hull machine-gun and drawing its fuel from an armoured but jettisonable two-wheel trailer carrying 400 Imp gal (1,818 litres) of fuel and compressed nitrogen propellant.

the cast vertical sections and, perhaps most importantly, was the first British example of a commander's cupola providing a 360° field of vision in the closed-down mode. The close-support version of the Mk VII was the Churchill VIII, which was in fact the last production variant of the Churchill. This was identical to the Mk VII in all but its armament, which was the same as that of the Mk V: one 94mm (3.7in) howitzer and two 7.92mm (0.312in) Besa machine-guns (one co-axial and the other in the bow plate).

The last three marks were earlier Churchills reworked to improved standards with appliqué armour and the cast turret of the Mk VII complete with the 75mm (2.95in) gun. The designations Churchill IX, X and XI were used for Mks III and IV, Mk VI and Mk V tanks respectively, while the suffix LT (light turret) was used for those that retained their original turrets (revised for the heavier main gun) but featured appliqué armour.

The roomy nature of the Churchill's hull combined with its reliability and good cross-country performance to promote its use for a large number of specialist roles. Several of these developments failed to pass the experimental stage, or to achieve more than very limited use, but others were important armoured vehicles that paved the way for future developments and additionally played a key part in the success of the British forces' final offensives against Germany. The Churchill AVRE (Armoured Vehicle Royal Engineers) was a specialist conversion of Mk III and Mk IV gun tanks to the standard required for assault engineer operations: the standard gun was replaced by an 11.42in (290mm) Petard spigot mortar, which could fire its 40lb (18.14kg) 'Flying Dustbin' bomb over an effective range of 80yds (75m) for the clearance of obstacles; the interior of the tank was stripped of gun-tank appurtenances to allow storage of special assault engineer stores, and the hull front was fitted with attachment points for special equipment. The Churchill Mk II SBG AVRE (Standard Box Girder Armoured Vehicle Royal Engineers) was a 1943 Canadian development of the Churchill AVRE with a 34ft (10.36m) box girder bridge on quick-release mountings. The bridge was controlled from a winch at the rear of the vehicle, and when faced with high obstacles, the practice was for one Mk II SGB AVRE to place its bridge at an angle against the obstacle and pull back, allowing a second vehicle carrying fascines to climb the ramp before dropping its fascines on the far side of the obstacle and then proceeding down them. The Churchill was also developed as a straightforward armoured vehicle-launched bridgelayer in forms such as the Churchill ARK and as the carrier and launcher for mobile and Bailey bridges.

To cross sand and heavy concentrations of obstacle-laced barbed wire, the Churchill was developed as a carpet-layer with one wide or two narrow strips of matting carried on arm-supported rollers in front of the tank. When required, the weighted end of the matting was dropped to the ground, the tank then moving forward over the matting which unrolled automatically; the spent bobbin was then discarded. Another obstacle-clearing device was the highly feared flamethrower, and the Churchill was developed in initial Churchill Oke and later Churchill Crocodile forms with this weapon. The Oke had an internal fuel tank for the flamethrower, but the Crocodile used a 400 Imp gal (1,818 litre) two-wheel trailer tank that could be jettisoned. In both cases the flame gun was carried in addition to the main gun armament, that of the Crocodile being a trainable weapon located in the position of the bow machine-gun for firing jets to a maximum range of 120yds (110m) although a more practical range was 80yds (75m).

Minefields were extensively laid by the Germans to hinder and channel the advance of the Allied armies, and all combatants developed their own systems to deal with this threat. So far as the Churchill was concerned, the type was trialled or used with roller, plough and explosive devices. Light obstacles were also a problem to the Allies, and the Churchill carried mechanical charge placers such as the Light Carrot, Jones Onion, Goat, and Bangalore Torpedo. Finally, in the Churchill story, come the Churchill 3in Gun Carrier Mk I and the A43 Infantry Tank Black Prince. The gun carrier was a self-propelled mounting for the 3in (76.2mm) Mk 3 AA gun in a limited-traverse mounting in the heightened front plate that now formed the forward edge of the box-like superstructure. The type was developed as an emergency measure in the days after Dunkirk, but the 50 production examples were delivered only from July 1942. The A43 was designed between 1943 and 1945 by Vauxhall as an enlarged version of the Churchill with a turret large enough to carry the 17pdr (3in/76.2mm) gun, and protection to the same scale as that of second-generation Churchills. The type was unofficially known as the Super Churchill, and was powered by the same Bedford unit as the standard Churchill: the weight was 112,000lb (50,803kg), and performance was notably low.

A27 Cruiser Tank Mk VIII Cromwell

Specification: A27M Cruiser Tank Mk VIII Cromwell IV

Country of origin: UK

Type: Cruiser tank

Crew: Five

Combat weight: 61,600lb (27,942kg)

Dimensions: Length, gun forward 21ft 0.75in (6.42m) and hull 20ft 5.5in (6.24m); width 10ft 0in (3.05m); height over aerial mountings 8ft 2in (2.49m)

Armament system: One 75mm (2.95in) QF Mk V or VA L/36.5 rifled gun with 64 rounds, two 7.92mm (0.312in) Besa machine-guns (one co-axial and one bow) with 4,952 rounds, two 0.303in (7.7mm) Vickers Type K or Bren AA machine-guns with 2,000 or 600 rounds respectively, one 2in (50.8mm) bomb thrower with 30 rounds, and two smoke-dischargers on each side of the hull rear; the turret was hydraulically operated, the main gun was stabilised in neither elevation (-12.5° to +20°) nor azimuth (360°), and simple optical sights were fitted

Armour: Riveted, welded and cast steel varying in thickness between 0.315 and 3in (8 and 76mm)

Powerplant: One 600hp (447.4kW) Rolls-Royce Meteor petrol engine with 116 Imp gal (527 litres) of fuel

Performance: Speed, road 38mph (61.2km/h); range, road 173 miles (278km); fording 3ft 0in (0.91m) without preparation or 4ft 0in (1.22m) with preparation; gradient 47%; vertical obstacle 3ft 0in (0.91m); trench 7ft 6in (2.29m); ground clearance 16in (0.41m)

The 6pdr (57mm) gun was beginning to mature as a weapon in 1940 although it entered production only in 1941 because of the need to keep the current 2pdr (40mm) gun in production. The 6pdr (57mm) gun offered the firepower required for the new generation of cruiser tanks, so the main problem to be addressed was the deficiency in protection. By 1940 the War Office had decided on its next move, and early in 1941 issued a requirement for a new heavy cruiser tank to be called the Cromwell.

This requirement demanded armour on a 2.75in (70mm) basis, thereby offering some 50 per cent more protection than that available on the Crusader, and a 6pdr (57mm) main armament in a turret using a turret ring of 60in (1.524m) diameter so that there would be adequate turret volume for the commander, gunner and loader. The requirement specified a combat weight of about 56,000lb (25,401kg) for the new tank, which was to be powered by a Rolls-Royce Meteor (a derivative of the Merlin aero engine) to provide cruiser-type performance. The stumbling block to rapid progress was the engine, which was still at an early stage of development by Leyland and Rolls-Royce. As an interim measure, therefore, Nuffield Mechanisations and Aero was commissioned to produce the A24 Cruiser Tank Mk VII with the hull and turret of the proposed Cromwell but the power train and other mechanical features of the Crusader. The type was initially called the Cromwell I, but this was soon changed to Cavalier. The design was ordered into production 'off the drawing board' to the extent 500 tanks, and the prototype appeared in January 1942. This 59,360lb (26,926kg) vehicle was powered by a 410hp (306kW) Liberty engine, but was so grossly underpowered that consistent use of the maximum 24mph (38.6km/h) speed resulted in frequent engine failures. The Cavalier was never used in action as a gun tank, but served with modest success for training, and with greater success as the basis of specialist derivatives such as an observation-post vehicle for the Royal Artillery. Perhaps most importantly of all, the tank's lack of success finally persuaded the War Office to cease its practice of ordering tanks 'off the drawing board'.

Continued delays with the Meteor engine led to a second interim model, the A27L Cruiser Tank Mk VIII Centaur, which was originally called the Cromwell II until it was decided to retain the name 'Cromwell' exclusively for the definitive Meteor-engine variant. The Centaur first appeared in prototype form in June 1942, and was in effect a Cromwell tank apart from its use of a 395hp (295kW) Liberty engine, and since the type was designed with an engine compartment that could accept either engine, many Centaurs were re-engined with the Meteor to become Cromwell Xs. Primary design responsibility for the Centaur

was allocated in November 1941 to Leyland rather than Nuffield Mechanisations and Aero, and the comparatively superior reliability and success of the Centaur resulted in Leyland becoming 'parent' to the Cromwell development and production programme in succession to the Birmingham Railway Carriage and Wagon Company, which had accepted temporary parentage in September 1941.

The Centaur weighed 61,600lb (27,942kg) and attained a speed of 27mph (43.5km/h), and was similar to the Cavalier in protection and armament: protection varied from a minimum of 0.79in (20mm) to a maximum of 3in (76mm), and in the initial Centaur I and Centaur II variants the armament comprised one 6pdr (57mm) gun plus one or two 7.92mm (0.312in) Besa machine-guns located as one co-axial weapon and one optional bow weapon. The Centaur III introduced a 75mm (2.95in) Mk 5 gun in place of the 6pdr (57mm) weapon, and the Centaur IV was the close-support model with a 94mm (3.7in) Tank Howitzer Mk 1.

The scene was finally set for the A27M Cruiser Tank

Fast as a result of its 600hp (447kW) Rolls-Royce Meteor engine and well armed with a high-velocity 75mm (2.95in) gun, the Cromwell cruiser tank was initially of riveted construction but later had a larger measure of welded fabrication for greater strength and improved protection. The type's main failing was the large number of vertical surfaces, especially on the turret.

Mk VIII Cromwell, the suffix to the A-series designation indicating that this was the Meteor- rather than Liberty-engined variant of the basic A27 type. Development had been very protracted, in part because of delays with the Meteor engine and in part to the exhaustive evaluation programme demanded by the War Office after the problems with the Crusader and Cavalier production runs. Although the first Cromwell prototype had run in January 1942, it was January 1943 before the first Cromwell I gun tanks began to come off the production line. The first vehicles had the 600hp (447kW) Meteor engine built by Rolls-Royce, although production of this important tank engine was switched as rapidly as possible to other sources so that Rolls-Royce could concentrate on its aero engine development and production programmes. The availability of the new engine finally gave British tanks the performance fillip they so desperately needed: there was now great reliability and ample power, and the engine rarely needed to be run be run at the high power settings that had caused the less powerful Liberty to break down so regularly.

The Cromwell had been planned with the 6pdr (57mm) gun, but during 1942 there was a gradual switch in user preference from the dedicated anti-tank gun to a dual-capable weapon capable of firing anti-tank and HE rounds. Officers with experience of the American M3 Grant and M4 Sherman tanks were unanimous in their praise for the 75mm (2.95in) M2 and M3 weapons used in these vehicles, and their pressure finally convinced the War Office. In January 1943 it was decided that the majority of medium tanks should be fitted with a dual-capable weapon, and should be supported in action by smaller numbers of tanks with role-specific anti-tank and close-support weapons. The result in the armament field was the rapid creation of the 75mm (2.95in) Mk 5/5A gun using many parts from the 6pdr (57mm) gun and firing the standard range of US ammunition for the M2/M3 gun. The British 75mm (2.95in) gun was derived from the 6pdr (57mm) weapon; with the barrel bored out, shortened and fitted with a single-baffle muzzle brake: it weighed 692lb (314kg), and the L/36.5 barrel fired the 13.75lb (6.24kg) projectile with a muzzle velocity of 2,030ft (619m) per second. Several other types of projectile could be carried, adding considerably to the tactical versatility of the tank, and as well as a capable HE projectile these included an anti-tank type that could penetrate 2.68in (68mm) of armour at an angle of 30° at a range of 500yds (457m).

It was therefore planned to fit this weapon in the Cromwell, whose generous turret-ring diameter made such a move possible without undue modification. But as the weapon did not become available until October 1943, the first Cromwells were delivered with the 6pdr (57mm) gun. In overall configuration the Cromwell was similar to the Cavalier and Centaur, and thus of typical British tank layout. The construction was of armour plates of varying thicknesses riveted together, although some variants of the Mks V and VII had all-welded hulls, the suffix 'w' being added to the designation in these cases. The forward compartment was occupied by the driver and bow machine-gunner, the centrally located turret (traversed by hydraulic power) provided accommodation for the commander, gunner and loader/radio operator in a turntable basket that moved with the turret, and the rear compartment contained the engine and transmission to the rear drive sprockets. The Christie running gear was derived from that of the A13 with suitable strengthening, and comprised five large and independently sprung road wheels but no track-return rollers; the idler was at the front. The transmission included a Merritt-Brown combined gearbox and steering unit of the type validated in the Churchill infantry tank, and this provided driving flexibility, reliability and maintenance simplicity far superior to the Merritt-Maybach system used in most American and German tanks.

The Cromwell remained in service until 1950, and went through an extensive development programme. The Cromwell I was the baseline model and had an armament of one 6pdr (57mm) gun and two 7.92mm (0.312in) Besa machine-guns. The Cromwell II was similar to the Mk I but was fitted with tracks 15.5in (394mm) rather than 14in (356mm) wide to reduce ground pressure and thus promote agility in poor conditions. The Cromwell III was originally designated Cromwell X, and was produced by converting the Centaur I with the Meteor engine. The Cromwell IV was the result of a similar process, and was produced by converting the Centaur III with the Meteor engine and a 75mm (2.95in) gun. The Cromwell V marked a significant improvement in the basic tank as it was the first production model to be fitted with the 75mm (2.95in) gun; there was also a Cromwell Vw with a welded rather than riveted hull. The Cromwell VI was a close-support version fitted with a 94mm (3.7in) howitzer in place of the 75mm (2.95in) gun. The Cromwell VII was based on the Mk IV but was fitted with wider tracks, a reduced ratio final drive to decrease maximum speed from 40 to 32mph (64.4 to 51.5km/h), and had increased armour thicknesses including the upgrading of the frontal protection to 3.98in (101mm), thereby increasing combat weight to 62,720lb (28,450kg); there was also a Cromwell VIIw variant with the welded hull. And the final production variant was the Cromwell VIII, which was essentially the Cromwell VI close-support version with the improvements of the Cromwell VII.

There were several subvariants designated by the suffixes 'D' (a side-opening door for the hull gunner), 'E' (final drive ratio altered from 4.5:1 to 3.7:1), and 'F' (a side-opening door for the driver).

The Cromwell proved itself an excellent tank in terms of protection and mobility, and when properly handled could evade the more powerfully armed German tanks.

KV

Specification: KV-85

Country of origin: USSR

Type: Heavy tank

Crew: Four

Combat weight: 103,042lb (46,740kg)

Dimensions: Length, gun forward 28ft 10.75in (8.50m) and hull 22ft 3.75in (6.80m); width 10ft 8in (3.25m); height 9ft 6.25in (2.90m)

Armament system: One 85mm (3.35in) gun with 71 rounds and three 7.62mm (0.3in) DT machine-guns with 3,276 rounds

Armour: Cast and welded steel varying in thickness between 1.18 and 4.33in (30 and 110mm)

Powerplant: One 447kW (600hp) V-2K-s diesel engine with 121 Imp gal (550 litres) of fuel

Performance: Speed, road 21.75mph (35km/h); range, road 155 miles (250km); fording 5ft 3in (1.6m); gradient 36%; vertical obstacle 3ft 11.25in (1.2m); trench 8ft 10.25in (2.7m); ground clearance 15.75in (0.4m)

The Soviets were long-term advocates of the heavy tank, and during the 1930s travelled along much the same design path as the heavy tank advocates of other countries until they

The KV series of heavy tanks was derived from the preceding T-100 and SMK vehicles with superfiring turrets for their 76.2 and 45mm (3 and 1.77in) main guns, but the KV-1 switched to a more orthodox single turret with one 76.2mm (3in) gun.

reached the massive T-100 and SMK types with their main turrets on barbettes to give them a superfiring capability over the auxiliary turret. The fallacy of this practice was fully revealed in the Russo-Finnish 'Winter War' (1939-40), when these slow-moving and clumsy vehicles proved highly susceptible to successful engagement by the Finns' artillery. Yet at the beginning of World War II in 1939 the USSR was the only country to have placed such monsters into full-scale production, the initial type being the KV-1 named for Marshal of the Soviet Union Klimenti Voroshilov. Design of the KV-1 began during February 1939 at the Kirov factory in Leningrad, the intention of the design team being a heavy tank with less height than its predecessors, and therefore overcoming their stability and visibility problems. The KV-1 was modelled on the T-100 and SMK (especially in the design and structure of the hull, and the nature of the running gear with torsion bar suspension), but without the auxiliary turret and its 45mm gun, thereby removing the need for the main turret's barbette and allowing a general reduction in overall dimensions and weight.

The prototype KV-1 was built between April and September 1939, and the type was ordered into production at the same time as the T-34 medium tank in December of the same year. The machine had a crew of five, and at a

weight of 104,719lb (47,500kg) with a maximum 3.03in (77mm) thickness of hull armour attained a speed of 21.75mph (35km/h) on its 600hp (447kW) V-2K diesel engine. The massive turret was made of welded armour between 1.18 and 2.95in (30 and 75mm) thick with a 0.98in (25mm) cast mantlet, and was fitted with the same 76.2mm (3in) main armament as the T-34/76; the secondary armament comprised three 7.62mm (0.3in) machine-guns.

The KV-1 entered production in Leningrad in February 1940, and some 245 had been produced by the end of the year. A few were sent for operational evaluation in the Finnish campaign, proving successful in the breakthrough of the Finns' Mannerheim Line defences. After the German invasion of June 1941 and the subsequent advance of the German forces deep into western Russia, the Kirov factory was evacuated to Chelyabinsk, where all subsequent production was undertaken (to the extent of 13,500 chassis used for assault guns as well as heavy tanks). Variants of the KV-1 were the KV-1A of 1940 with the L/41.2 main gun, resilient road wheels, an additional 0.79in (20mm) of armour on the nose, and a cast mantlet with 0.98in (25mm) welded armour strengthening; the KV-1B of 1941 with an additional 0.98 to 1.38in (25 to 35mm) of armour bolted and later welded to the hull front and sides, and later with a cast turret increasing weight to 107,520lb (48,771kg); the KV-1C of 1942 with the cast turret, wider tracks, an uprated engine and maximum armour thicknesses increased to 5.12in (130mm) on the hull and 4.72in (120mm) on the turret; and the KV-1s (*skorostnoy*, or fast) of 1942 with weight reduced to 95,205lb (43,185kg) by the omission of the appliqué armour, to increase speed from 21.2 to 27.7mph (34 to 44.5km/h).

Running in parallel with KV-1 production was that of the KV-2 artillery fire-support version with an enormous slab-sided turret accommodating a 152mm (6in) howitzer. The size of this turret was a severe tactical hindrance, as too was the weight of 118,717lb (53,850kg) without any increase in power, and the KV-2's short production life was mirrored by its brief operational career. It had been planned to develop a KV-3 heavy tank on the same basic chassis but fitted with a turret able to accept a 107mm (4.21in) gun, but this did not proceed past the prototype stage, so the final variant of this family was the KV-85 of 1943 with a large cast turret for an 85mm (3.35in) gun. Most KV-85s were produced by converting KV-1s at a weight of 103,064lb (46,750kg).

Medium Tank M3 Lee and Grant

Specification: Medium Tank M3 (Lee Mk I)

Country of origin: USA

Type: Medium tank

Crew: Six

Combat weight: 60,000lb (27,216kg)

Dimensions: Length overall 18ft 6in (5.64m); width 8ft 11in (2.72m); height overall 10ft 3in (3.12m)

Armament system: One 75mm (2.95in) M2 L/28.47 or M3 L/37.5 rifled gun with 46 rounds in a right-hand hull sponson allowing gyro-stabilised elevation in an unspecified arc and azimuth movement of 60°, one 37mm M5 L/50 or M6 L/55 gun with 178 rounds, and four 0.3in (7.62mm) Browning M1919A4 machine-guns (one co-axial, two bow and one AA) with 9,200 rounds; the turret was hydraulically operated (with manual reversion), the 37mm gun was gyro-stabilised in elevation through an unspecified arc but not in azimuth (360°), and simple optical sights were fitted

Armour: Riveted steel varying in thickness between 0.5 and 2.25in (12.7 and 57mm)

Powerplant: One 340hp (253.5kW) Continental R-975-EC2 or C1 petrol engine with 154 Imp gal (700 litres) of fuel

Performance: Speed, road 26mph (41.8km/h); range, road 120 miles (193km); fording 3ft 4in (1.01m); gradient 60%; vertical obstacle 2ft 0in (0.61m); trench 6ft 2.5in (1.89m); ground clearance 17in (0.43m)

Although the US Army developed and used light tanks in large numbers during the 1930s, and indeed maintained their use of the Light Tanks M3 and M5 into the closing stages of World War II, it was aware throughout the 1930s that this was a matter of economic necessity rather than military desirability. The service therefore had its sights firmly set on a medium tank series that would be the mainstay of its armoured divisions in World War II. In the late 1930s the US Army's principal vehicle in this class was the Medium Tank M2 and basically similar M2A1 armed with a 37mm main gun, but in 1940 it was realised that, despite their recent development, these vehicles were obsolete by the standard now set by German tank development and operations. In August 1940, therefore, the heads of the Armored Force and the Ordnance Department decided on the specification for a new medium tank with armour on a 1.5in (38mm) basis and a 75mm (2.95in) main gun. So far as these features were concerned the specification was adequate, but it was realised that the US Army had lagged behind the European nations in developing large-diameter turrets of the type required for a 75mm (2.95in) gun, and that an alternative installation would have to be considered. Such a mounting had already been trialled in a Medium Tank T5 Phase III (the final precursor of the M2), which had been fitted with a 75mm (2.95in) pack howitzer in a limited-traverse mounting carried in a sponson on the right-hand side of the hull. It was decided, therefore, to upgrade the M2 with thicker armour and a 75mm (2.95in) sponson-mounted gun in addition to the existing 37mm weapon (in a cast rather than welded turret surmounted by a secondary turret accommodating the commander and a 0.3in/7.62mm machine-gun) as the new Medium Tank M3.

Late in August 1940, a recently-placed order for 1,000 M2A1s was modified to the same number of M3s in a programme co-ordinated by William Knudsen (president of the General Motors Corporation and a co-opted member of the National Defense Advisory Committee). It was Knudsen who was largely instrumental in persuading the US military authorities that tank production was better entrusted to the car industry than to the heavy engineering industry (in the forms of the American Locomotive Company (Alco) and the Baldwin Locomotive Company for medium tanks), and production of the new M3 was allocated to a new government-owned facility run by the Chrysler Corporation.

The key to the new tank was the M2 gun, a 783lb (355kg) weapon derived by the Watervliet Arsenal from the celebrated French Modèle 1897 field gun. This weapon was 91.75in (2.33m) long, and its L/28.5 barrel allowed the 14.96lb (6.79kg) armour-piercing projectile to be fired with a muzzle velocity of 1,860ft (567m) per second, providing an armour-penetration capability of 2.36in (60mm) angled at 30° at a range of 500yds (457m): this translated as a 25 per

This M3A1 reveals the salient features of the Medium Tank M3 series, especially the 75mm (2.95in) main gun in the starboard-side sponson and the 37mm gun

cent improvement over the capabilities of the 37mm M6 gun, and the M2 could also fire a useful HE round. The M2 was an interim model, the definitive weapon in this calibre being the M3 weighing 910lb (413kg) and measuring 118.375in (3.01m) in overall length: this had an L/37.5 barrel, which gave the standard armour-piercing projectile a muzzle velocity of 2,300ft (701m) per second for an armour-penetration capability of 2.76in (70mm) at an angle of 30° at a range of 500yds (457m). The M3 gun was ready for installation on later M3 tanks, and was also earmarked for the M3's successor, the legendary M4. The primary limitation of the 75mm (2.95in) gun mounting in the M3 was its small traverse (15° left and right of the centreline), while a useful feature was the provision (for the first time in an operational tank) of a Westinghouse stabilisation system for the main and secondary guns in elevation. This allowed moderately accurate fire even with the tank on the move, a feature impossible with shoulder- or gear-controlled guns. In tactical terms, the location of the main gun in a sponson meant that much of the tank's considerable height had to be exposed to bring the gun into action, while the engagement of targets more than 15° off the centreline meant manoeuvring the whole vehicle.

Prototypes of the new M3 were delivered in January

1941 by Chrysler, additional vehicles following from Alco and Baldwin by April. Production was launched in August 1941, and 6,258 M3s were built before production ceased in December 1942: 3,352 came from Chrysler, and smaller numbers from Alco, Baldwin, Pressed Steel and Pullman, fully vindicating the decision to allocate the bulk of medium tank production to the car industry.

The six-man M3 bore a marked similarity to the M2, retaining from its predecessor the massive and angular hull, the aero engine-derived powerplant, and the running gear that comprised on each side three twin-wheel bogies with vertical volute spring suspension, three track-return rollers (located at the upper end of each bogie attachment), a front drive sprocket and a rear idler. Given the fact that the 51,520lb (23,369kg) M2A1 was powered by a 400hp (298kW) Wright radial engine, the M3 had only a 340hp (253.5kW) version of the same unit to move its 60,000lb (27,216kg) mass, which resulted in a maximum speed of 26mph (41.8km/h) rather than the 30mph (48.3km/h) of the M2A1.

The M3 entered US service in 1941; it was also delivered in substantial numbers to the British under the terms of the Lend-Lease programme, mostly for service in North Africa and the Far East. Although the M3 medium tank's production life was comparatively short, several important variants appeared, reflecting the rapid pace of development in the first half of World War II and also the ability of American manufacturing companies to respond to these developments without undue delay.

The original M3 (General Lee I in British service) had a riveted hull and a Wright R-975 radial petrol engine, though some M3 (Diesel) tanks were fitted with a Guiberson T-1400 diesel engine to overcome shortages of the Wright engine. Next came the M3A1 (General Lee II), mechanically identical to the M3 with Wright or Guiberson engines but built exclusively to the extent of 300 vehicles by Alco, the only company in the programme able to produce this variant's cast upper hull whose side hatches were later eliminated to provide extra strength, an escape hatch then being added in the belly. The M3A2 was not used by the British, though the designation General Lee III had been allocated, and the variant was mechanically identical to the M3 but was based on a welded rather than riveted hull. M3A2 production amounted to only 12 vehicles before Baldwin switched to the 63,000lb (28,577kg) M3A3 (General Lee IV) with a welded hull and completely revised powerplant. This powerplant comprised two General Motors 6-71 diesel engines coupled to deliver 375hp (280kW): the larger engine installation reduced fuel capacity from 145.7 to 124.9 Imp gal (662 to 568 litres), but the efficiency of the diesel powerplant boosted range from 120 to 160 miles (193 to 257km). Production was by Baldwin to a total of 322 vehicles, and some British-operated M3A3s were re-engined with the Wright radial and given the designation General Lee V. The M3A4 (General Lee VI) was identical to the original M3 in everything but its engine, which was a 370hp (276kW) Chrysler A-57 multi-bank petrol unit made by combining five car cylinder blocks on a common crankshaft; the engine was longer than the earlier units, and to provide an adequate engine compartment the hull had to be increased in length by 14in (0.356m) to an overall figure of 19ft 8in (5.99m), increasing weight to 64,000lb (29,030kg). Production of 109 vehicles was undertaken by Chrysler. The final production variant was the M3A5, identical to the M3A3 in every respect but its hull, which was riveted rather than welded for a weight of 64,000lb (29,030kg) and had the side doors either welded shut or eliminated: Baldwin delivered 591 such vehicles, the last of them with the longer M3 gun fitted with a counterbalance weight at the muzzle.

As noted above, tanks of the M3 series were delivered to the UK with the name General Lee. The British also bought a variant of the basic M3 with a number of modifications, as the General Grant. The most notable of these modifications was to the 360° traverse turret, which was lengthened to the rear so that a radio could be installed, and stripped of its secondary turret to reduce overall height. Similar modification was later made to the M3A5 to produce the General Grant II, whereupon the original variant became the General Grant I. It was as the General Grant that the type made its combat debut in the Battle of Gazala in May 1942, and when, for the first time, the British had a tank with a gun matching that of the Germans' PzKpfw IV. The importance of the Lee/Grant to the British was considerable, and although there were earlier problems with the fuses and filling of the type's HE shell, the tank played a significant part in the British success at the 2nd Battle of El Alamein in October and November 1942.

The M3 was of tactical importance in its own right, but was also of significance in buying time for the development of the Americans' most important medium tank of World War II.

Medium Tank M4 Sherman

Specification: Medium Tank M4A3E8 Sherman

Country of origin: USA

Type: Medium tank

Crew: Five

Combat weight: 71,175lb (32,285kg)

Dimensions: Length, gun forward 24ft 8in (7.513m) and hull 20ft 7in (6.273m); width 8ft 9in (2.667m); height to turret top 11ft 3in (3.43m)

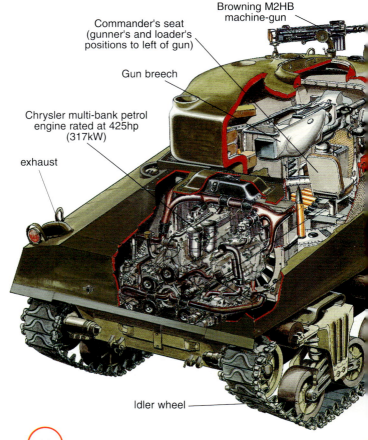

Browning M2HB machine-gun

Commander's seat (gunner's and loader's positions to left of gun)

Gun breech

Chrysler multi-bank petrol engine rated at 425hp (317kW)

exhaust

Idler wheel

Armament system: One 3in (76.2mm) M1A1/2 rifled gun with 71 rounds, two 0.3in (7.62mm) Browning M1919A4 machine-guns (one co-axial and one bow) with 6,250 rounds, and one 0.5in (12.7mm) Browning M2HB AA machine-gun with 600 rounds; the turret was hydraulically powered, the main gun was stabilised in neither elevation (-10° to +25°) nor azimuth (360°), and an optical fire-control system was fitted

Armour: Cast and welded steel varying in thickness between 1 and 3in (25.4 and 76.2mm)

Powerplant: One 450hp (336kW) Ford GAA petrol engine with 140 Imp gal (636 litres) of fuel

Performance: Speed, road 30mph (48km/h); range, road 100 miles (161km); fording 3ft 0in (0.91m); gradient 60%; vertical obstacle 2ft 0in (0.61m); trench 7ft 5in (2.26m); ground clearance 17in (0.43m)

The Americans had appreciated from the beginning of the M3 programme that the sponson-mounted main gun of this medium tank was a potent tactical limitation, and on 29 August 1940 (just one day after the first production order for the M3 had been placed) design work began on an M3 successor with its 75mm (2.95in) main gun in a 360° traverse turret: this would provide great tactical improvements, while the elimination of a sponson reduced the volume requiring armour protection, thereby allowing a lighter weight of armour for a more sprightly vehicle or, more practically, greater weight of armour over the protected volume that now accommodated five rather than six men. As much as possible of the M3 was retained, and the result was the

Track with 79 separate shoes

Vertical volute spring suspension unit with two rubber-tyred road wheels

The Medium Tank M4 Sherman, seen here in M4A4 form, was the most important armoured fighting vehicle operated by the Western Allies in World War II. The Sherman was limited in a number of respects, but its reliability and availability in very large numbers more than offset any limitations.

Medium Tank T6 development model with a short-barrel M2 gun in a cast turret on a cast hull. The machine weighed 67,200lb (30,482kg), was powered by a 400hp (298kW) Wright radial engine for a speed of 26mph (41.8km/h), and in addition to its main gun possessed an armament of four 0.3in (7.62mm) machine-guns located as one co-axial, one bow and two fixed forward-firing nose guns. Prototype vehicles were delivered in September 1941, and trials confirmed the ex-pectations of the designers and the army: in October 1941 a slightly modified version of the T6 (with a belly hatch and an additional driver's hatch in place of the side doors) was standardised as the Medium Tank M4 (the name 'Sherman' was bestowed initially by the British within their system of naming US tanks after famous American generals). The M4 was planned to supersede the M3 on all current medium tank production lines, with additional sources coming on stream as production increased. It was then realised that adequate casting facilities were not available for the anticipated number of hulls (at one time planned as 2,000 vehicles per month), and a box-like upper hull of welded construction was developed as an alternative.

Vehicles with the welded hull were designated M4, and those with the cast hull M4A1: both used the same one-piece cast turret, which had a maximum frontal thickness of 3in (76mm), an Oilgear hydraulic or Westinghouse electric power traverse system, and a stabilisation system for the main gun in elevation. The main gun was the longer-barrel M3 weapon rather than the M2 used in the T6.

In overall layout the Sherman was typical of its era, with a forward compartment for the driver and co-driver/nose gunner (the two fixed guns of the T6 being abandoned as superfluous soon after the M4A1's production life had begun), a central fighting compartment for the commander, gunner and loader, and a rear compartment for the engine. On each side, the running gear comprised three twin-wheel bogies with vertical volute spring suspension, three track-return rollers located one at the top of each bogie attachment unit ('first-type suspension'), a front drive sprocket and a rear idler. The standard engine was the 400hp (298kW) Wright R-975 radial petrol engine.

The Sherman ran through a large number of variants and subvariants, and these are listed below in order of designation rather than production by the M3

The main features of the Medium Tank M4 Sherman were a well-proved lower element based on that of the Medium Tank M3 Lee/Grant series, and a new but carefully considered turret capable of traverse through 360° and carrying an effective main gun.

manufacturers, who were joined by Federal Machine and Welder, Fisher Body, the Ford Motor Company, and Pacific Car and Foundry. First in the designation sequence was the M4, designated Sherman I by the British: 8,389 of this model were built, 6,748 of them with the standard 75mm (2.95in) M3 gun and the other 1,641 with the 105mm (4.13in) M4 howitzer for use in the close-support role; the British designated the latter version the Sherman IB, and the suffix 'B' was used thereafter to denote Shermans with the howitzer. The M4 was a very useful weapon, and was fitted in a mounting that allowed elevation to a maximum of 35° rather than the 25° of the M3 gun: the ordnance weighed 973lb (441kg) and was 101.3in (2.57m) long, its L/22.5 barrel firing a 33lb (14.97kg) HE shell (or alternative HEAT and Smoke projectiles) to give the projectile a muzzle velocity of 1,550ft (472m) per second.

The M4 was standardised in October 1941 but became only the third model to go into production, and was distinguishable by its all-welded hull. Early production models had a differential housing comprising three cast sections bolted together, and later models (designated Hybrid Sherman I by the British) had a combination cast and rolled hull front together with a one-piece cast differential housing. This evolution of the hull front and differential was also a characteristic of other Sherman variants.

Next in designation sequence, but actually the first to enter production, was the M4A1 (Sherman II) with a cast hull. During the course of production the M4A1 received differential and hull front modifications parallel to those of the M4, and the track-return rollers were later shifted to the rear of the bogie attachment units ('second-type suspension'). Like the M4, the combat weight was 66,500lb (30,164kg). Production of this variant amounted to 9,677 tanks, of which 6,281 were completed with the M3 gun and the other 3,396 with the 76.2mm (3in) M1 high-velocity gun, whose installation was signified in British terminology by the designation Sherman IIA. This gun resulted from the realisation by both the Armored Force and the Ordnance Department that the M3 was comparatively indifferent in armour-penetration capability by comparison with the guns of contemporary German tanks, which were also appearing with thicker armour.

The M1 gun was evolved in two months from an anti-aircraft weapon, and was tested during September 1942 in a standard M4 turret. This proved too small for the more powerful weapon, which was then installed in the cylindrical turret designed for the 90mm (3.54in) gun of the Medium Tank T23. This turret proved excellent, and could be installed on the M4 without modification. The gun/turret combination was authorised for the M4A3 in February 1944, deliveries beginning in the following month; the gun/turret combination was also used on the M4, M4A1 and M4A2, all signified in British usage by the suffix 'A' after the roman mark number. The M1 weighed 1,141lb (518kg) and was 163.75in (4.16m) long, its L/52 barrel giving the 15.4lb (6.98kg) APCR shot a muzzle velocity of 3,400ft (1,036m) per second for an armour-penetration capability of 102mm (4in) at a range of 1,000yds (915m).

The M4A2 was called Sherman III or Sherman IIIA by the British, depending on armament, and after standardisation in December 1941 became the second Sherman variant to enter production. The type was basically similar to the M4 with a welded hull, but had a different powerplant in the form of a 410hp (306kW) General Motors 6046 diesel engine, comprising two General Motors 6-71 diesel units geared to a common propeller shaft, giving this 69,000lb (31,298kg) vehicle a 29mph (46.7km/h) maximum speed in comparison

The M3-4-3 was a flamethrower version of the M4 Sherman, with the flame gun replacing the bow machine-gun and its fuel tank installed in the right-hand sponson.

to the 24mph (38.6km/h) speed of the two previously mentioned variants. Production amounted to 11,283 tanks, 8,053 of them with the 75mm (2.95in) gun and the other 3,230 with the 76.2mm (3in) gun. Late-production examples had a more-steeply inclined hull front that greatly simplified manufacture and also provided marginally better protection.

In January 1942 a new variant was standardised as the M4A3, which was designated Sherman IV by the British. This was again similar to the M4 with a welded hull, but was fitted with a custom-designed tank engine, the 500hp (373kW) Ford GAA. This powerful and reliable petrol unit was instrumental in making the M4A3 the most important single Sherman variant: 11,424 were built including 5,015 with the 75mm (2.95in) gun, 3,370 with the 76.2mm (3in) gun and the other 3,039 with the 105mm (4.13in) howitzer. Once the M4A3 was available, the Americans generally reserved this model for themselves and disbursed the types with other engines to their Lend-Lease allies. Included in the total of M4A3s with the 75mm (2.95in) gun were 254 examples of the special M4A3E2 variant, which was nicknamed 'Jumbo' and produced specifically for assault operations in the invasion of France during June 1944. It had been anticipated that in this invasion and the subsequent break-out operations the Allies would face heavy concentrations of powerful artillery and tank destroyers, so the 'Jumbo' was fitted with extra protection in the form of 4in (102mm) plate welded to the hull front, a new turret with 6in (152mm) frontal thickness, and rolled plate added to the hull top for a weight of 84,000lb (38,102kg) rather than the 68,500lb (31,072kg) of the standard M4A3, reducing maximum speed to 22mph (35.4km/h) on the 500hp (373kW) of the GAA engine. In the field, some 'Jumbos' were revised with the 76.2mm (3in) gun.

The M4A4 was called Sherman V by the British, and was indeed the main type supplied to the UK. The type was standardised in February 1942 as an M4 variant with a 425hp (317kW) Chrysler multi-bank engine created by marrying five car-engine cylinder blocks to a common crankcase. This was the same engine as used in the M3A4, and required a 6in (0.152m) lengthening of the rear hull and an additional four track shoes on each side. The type was phased out of production in September 1943, and all 7,499 examples had the 75mm (2.95in) gun and three-piece differential housing.

The designation M4A5 was used in the USA for the Canadian Ram tank, so the next production Sherman was the M4A6, which was designated Sherman VII by the British. The type was standardised in October 1943, and may be considered a variant of the M4A4 with the 497hp (371kW) Caterpillar D-200A diesel engine: the longer hull, widely spaced bogies, extended tracks and the 71,000lb (32,206kg) weight were retained, and the 75mm (2.95in) gun was standard. Production amounted to only 75 tanks, for at the end of 1943 it was decided to cease powerplant experimentation and concentrate all production effort on the Wright- and Ford-engined models. Total production of Sherman gun tanks was thus 48,347, but there were a large number of important variants produced by production-line, depot or even field modification.

The best known of these is perhaps the Sherman 'Firefly', a British conversion with the 17pdr (3in/76.2mm) high-velocity anti-tank gun (indicated by the suffix 'C') for enhanced tank-destroying capability. Most Fireflies were of the Sherman VC variety, but there were also Sherman IC, IIC, IIIC and IVC versions, and the family proved highly important in the Normandy and subsequent North-West European campaigns as the Allied tanks best able to tackle the Panther and Tiger on anything approaching an equal firepower footing. For installation in the Sherman turret, the 17pdr (3in/76.2mm) gun had to be turned on its side and adapted for left-hand loading, and was provided with new mounting, recoil and elevating gear. The long breech section of the gun occupied so much space that the radio had to be moved into an armoured box suspended from the rear of the turret, and this served the useful purpose of balancing the long barrel section of the gun. To provide maximum stowage for main armament ammunition, the bow machine-gun and its gunner's position were eliminated, allowing the accommodation of 78 rounds.

Other major modifications were less obvious but also important. Typical of these, and coincident with the sharply angled 47° hull front on the M4A3, was wet stowage for the main armament ammunition inside the vertical superstructure faces: the original stowage arrangement of dry racks had resulted in many disastrous fires and explosions, so the wet stowage used a hollow casing filled with a water/glycerine mixture to reduce the chance of combustion. Provision of such stowage was costly, both financially and in terms of manufacturing time, but proved well worth the expense. Another important change was horizontal rather than vertical volute spring suspension (indicated in US and British terminologies by the suffix 'E8' and 'Y' respectively): this was introduced to provide greater flotation and simplified maintenance, though the system's use of tracks that were 23in (584mm) rather than 16.5in (419mm) wide also did much to reduce ground pressure and so improve cross-country mobility in poor conditions. The horizontal suspension used bogies with four wheels arranged in lateral pairs, and the track-return rollers were attached directly to the hull sides. Field modifications were usually concerned with protection, and generally consisted of appliqué armour and additional track shoes welded to potentially vulnerable areas.

The Sherman was also used for a number of specialist roles, being developed in different forms by the Americans and the British to meet their particular requirements for armoured recovery vehicles, rocket-launchers, flame-throwers, mine exploders, self-propelled weapons and other role-dedicated vehicles. The Sherman proved as successful in these alternative roles as in its primary gun-tank role, and the importance of the tank in the Allied victory of World War II cannot be overemphasised. The Sherman may not have been a qualitative match for the best German tanks, but it was adequate to its tasks and was produced in the vast numbers that allowed Allied tank formations to overwhelm the Germans and, to a lesser extent, the Japanese. The Sherman remained in widespread service into the 1970s, and is still used by a number of armies.

Panzerkampfwagen III

Specification: PzKpfw III Ausf N (11/ZW) (SdKfz 141/2)

Country of origin: Germany

Type: Close-support medium tank

Crew: Five

Combat weight: 46,958lb (21,300kg)

Dimensions: Length overall 18ft 11.5in (5.78m) for production vehicles and 17ft 0.75in (5.52m) for Ausf L conversions; width 9ft 9.25in (2.97m) without skirts and 11ft 2.25in (3.41m) with skirts; height overall 8ft 2.5in (2.50m)

Armament system: One 75mm (2.95in) KwK L/24 rifled gun with 64 rounds in production vehicles and 56 rounds in Ausf L conversions, two 7.92mm (0.312in) MG 34 machine-guns (one co-axial and one bow) with 3,450 rounds, and six 90mm (3.54in) smoke-dischargers; the turret was manually operated, the main gun was stabilised in neither elevation (-8.3° to +20°) nor azimuth (360°), and simple optical sights were fitted

Armour: Welded steel varying in thickness between 0.63 and 2.76in (16 and 70mm) plus varying levels of additional armour

Powerplant: One 300hp (224kW) Maybach HL 120 TRM petrol engine with 70.4 Imp gal (320 litres) of fuel

Performance: Speed, road 24.9mph (40km/h); range, road 93.3 miles (155km); fording 2ft 7.5in (0.8m); gradient 57%; vertical obstacle 1ft 11.5in (0.6m); trench 7ft 2.5in (2.2m); ground clearance 15.2in (0.385m)

By 1935 the German designers and industrialists had gained sufficient experience with the PzKpfw I and PzKpfw II light tanks to embark with a realistic hope of success upon the first of Germany's two definitive battle tanks, the five-man PzKpfw III with a nominal weight of 15 tonnes. The German army's plan at this time was to field a force based on two main types, one a battle tank with a high-velocity anti-tank gun backed by machine-guns, and the other a medium tank with a medium-velocity gun backed by machine-guns and intended mainly for the support role: the battle tank became the PzKpfw III with a 37mm (later 50mm) gun, while the medium tank became the PzKpfw IV with a 75mm (2.95in) gun. The standard tank battalion had four companies, and it was planned that three of these would field the PzKpfw III battle tank.

Development of the battle tank was undertaken with the cover designation ZW, and prototype orders were placed with Daimler-Benz, Krupp, MAN and Rheinmetall during 1936. The Inspectorate for Mechanised Troops wished the ZW to be fitted with a 50mm gun, but the Ordnance Department pointed out that the infantry's standard anti-tank gun was a 37mm weapon: a compromise resulted in a decision that the type would carry the 37mm KwK L/45 gun, but would have a turret ring of adequate diameter to allow later substitution of the 50mm KwK 39 gun if tactical conditions altered. This was an extremely far-sighted move, and allowed the PzKpfw III to be retained as an effective weapon for about two years longer than would otherwise have been the case. It is inevitable that one should recall the A12 Matilda II, a potentially formidable British tank that could have played a decisive role if the turret ring had not been sized exactly to the 2pdr (40mm) tank gun of the late 1930s, and was thereby precluded from development with a larger-calibre gun of the type soon revealed to be essential.

It proved impossible to design a battle tank down to the desired limit of 15 tonnes, so the upper limit was raised to the 24-tonne rating of Germany's road bridges, and the selection battle settled down to a choice between Krupp and Daimler-Benz before the latter was selected for production of the PzKpfw III Ausf A (SdKfz 141) after features of the Krupp MKA prototype had been incorporated into the design. In overall layout the PzKpfw III followed the pattern finalised in the PzKpfw I with the driving compartment at the front, the fighting compartment in the centre and the engine compartment at the rear. The driver and radio operator/bow gunner were accommodated in the forward compartment, with the commander, gunner and loader in the fighting compartment/turret. The crew were favoured with considerable working space by

The PzKpfw III series was schemed in the 1930s as the primary battle tank of the German army's new force of highly mobile armoured divisions, and was planned with high performance in speed and mobility, good protection and adequate armament, although this last feature was deficient inasmuch as the turret ring was too small to permit upgunning from 37mm to more than 50mm.

comparison with contemporary tanks of the same basic type, and the driver had the useful advantage of a preselector gearbox: this required more maintenance than the crash gearbox used in most other tanks, but offered greater flexibility of operation in conjunction with the 230hp (171.5kW) Maybach HL 108 TR petrol engine. The drive sprockets were located at the front, the track on each side passing under the six coil-sprung road wheels before returning via the rear idler and two track-return rollers: this arrangement provided a good cross-country ride and a maximum speed of 19.9mph (32km/h). The sensible layout of the vehicle was echoed in the construction of high-grade chrome/molybdenum steel armour: the hull was a bolted-together assembly of three welded subassemblies (the lower hull, the forward upper hull and the rear upper hull), and the turret was another welded assembly. The minimum and maximum armour thicknesses in the prototype were 0.39 and 0.57in (10 and 14.5mm) respectively, resulting in a weight of 33,951lb (15,400kg). The armament rather let down the potential of the tank, being the 37mm KwK L/45 gun and three 7.92mm (0.312in) MG 34 machine-guns (two co-axial with the main armament and the third in the bow): the main gun had the useful ammunition stowage of 150 rounds, but its indifference as an anti-tank weapon is indicated by its ability to penetrate only 1.42in (36mm) of armour angled at 30° at a range of 545yds (500m) with its 1.65lb (0.75kg) shot fired at a muzzle velocity of 2,493ft (760m) per second.

The PzKpfw III Ausf A was a pre-production type, and only 10 were built before production switched to the PzKpfw III Ausf B in 1937. This was identical to the Ausf A in all respects except its running gear, which now consisted on each side of eight small road wheels: these were arranged in two-wheel bogies, which were supported in pairs by large horizontal leaf springs; there were also three track-return rollers. Production of this variant amounted to 15 tanks, which were supplanted by the PzKpfw III Ausf C in which the suspension was revised once more, in this instance so that each two-wheel bogie was supported by an individual leaf spring. The next pre-production variant was the PzKpfw III Ausf D, evolved from the Ausf C but with the armour increased to a 1.18in (30mm) basis: again, 15 of these 43,651lb (19,800kg) vehicles were built. The final pre-production model was the PzKpfw III Ausf E, which appeared in 1938. This had a more powerful engine in the form of the 320hp (239kW) Maybach HL 120 TR, a revised transmission and, most significant of all, new running gear. On each side this consisted of six road wheels independently sprung by transverse torsion bars.

At about this time the Ordnance Department finally appreciated its short-sightedness in pressing for a 37mm main armament, and instructed Krupp to proceed with the design of a new turret to accommodate the 50mm KwK 39 gun. The development had not been completed, however, when the next variant of the tank III was being readied for production in early 1940 as the PzKpfw III Ausf F. This 44,753lb (20,300kg) variant had to retain the 37mm gun, so its main improvements over the Ausf E included better ventilation, five smoke emitters on the rear decking, a stowage box on the turret, and the HL 120 TRM engine rated at 300hp (224kW). The new main armament was still not ready when the PzKpfw III Ausf G was introduced later in 1940, so this variant also retained the 37mm main gun. It had the same weight and improvements as the Ausf F, but also featured a revised commander's cupola with improved protection for the vision ports.

All three of these variants were retrofitted with the new KwK L/42 gun as this became available, to the annoyance of Hitler who appreciated the pace of armoured warfare development and thus demanded the longer and more powerful KwK 39 L/60 gun of the same calibre: firing the same round with a 4.52lb (2.05kg) shot, the L/42 weapon generated a muzzle velocity of 2,247ft (685m) per second, sufficient to penetrate 1.93in (49mm) of armour at an angle of 30° at a range of 545yds (500m), whereas the L/60 weapon generated a muzzle velocity of 2,707ft (825m) per second to penetrate 2.36in (60mm) of armour at the same inclination and range. Stowage of 50mm ammunition amounted to 99 rounds.

The PzKpfw III entered its stride as a production weapon with the PzKpfw III Ausf H, the main production variant in the period between late 1940 and the end of 1941. The first large-scale production variant, the PzKpfw III Ausf E, had been allocated for production to several companies with little experience in the manufacture of armoured fighting vehicles, and had suffered in terms of production quantity and quality because of the comparatively complex manufacturing techniques required: therefore the PzKpfw III Ausf H had features to ease mass production, the most important being new idlers and drive sprockets, and a transmission arrangement with a six-speed manual gearbox in place of the original 10-speed preselector box. As a result of combat experience in Poland and the Western campaign, extra protection was added in the form of bolt-on plates as well as a measure of spaced armour to defeat hollow-charge warheads. This boosted the PzKpfw III Ausf H's combat weight to 47,619lb (21,600kg), and to reduce ground pressure, 15.75in (400mm) tracks replaced the original 14.17in (360mm) tracks. The 300hp (224kW) Maybach HL 120 TRM petrol engine introduced on the Ausf E was used in this and all later variants. Early examples of the PzKpfw III Ausf H retained the 50mm KwK L/42 gun, but later examples were produced with the more capable KwK 39 L/60 weapon of the same calibre, and this was also retrofitted to tanks already in service.

By the beginning of the campaign against the USSR in June 1941 some 1,500 PzKpfw III tanks were in service, and these performed creditably in the opening stages of the campaign. The experience of the crews and the relative maturity of the basic design swept Soviet armour away without difficulty. But from the end of 1941 the new breed of Soviet tanks, epitomised by the T-34 medium and KV heavy types, began to appear in growing numbers: the Soviet tanks crews were now of better tactical quality, and the protection of their vehicles proved too thick for effective penetration by the L/42 gun. A crash programme was launched to retrofit the German tanks with the L/60 gun, which entailed a reduction in ammunition capacity from 99 to 84 rounds. To the dismay of the German authorities, this longer version of the 50mm gun also proved inadequate to the task of tackling the T-34 and KV tanks, except at the point-blank ranges that were seldom achievable on the Eastern Front. A longer-term implication was that Hitler, on learning that his earlier instructions to fit the L/60 weapon had not been obeyed immediately, started to take a more personal interest in the design and manufacture of German tanks, as well as in their deployment and tactical use.

The comparatively small diameter of the PzKpfw III's turret ring now proved the decisive factor in developing a more capable variant: the 50mm Krupp gun never proved entirely satisfactory, and the turret-ring diameter effectively prohibited the installation of a high-velocity gun of greater calibre. All the Germans could do, therefore, was to step up production of better-protected models in the hope that numbers would provide the Panzer arm with an edge over the Soviet tank force. It was an impossible task, and the PzKpfw III was rapidly overhauled in quality and quantity by Soviet production. At the same time, the German tank crews found themselves steadily matched in tactical capability by the USSR's increasingly experienced men. The next production variant was the PzKpfw III Ausf J, which was similar to the Ausf H apart from a reduction in hull and turret vision slots to ease manufacture, and an increase in armour protection from 1.18in (30mm) to 1.95in (50mm), resulting in an increase in weight to 49,162lb (22,300kg). The addition of another 1,543lb (700kg) of weight without any increase in installed power inevitably entailed a slight but significant degradation in cross-country performance and agility.

The next PzKpfw III variant was the PzKpfw III Ausf L,

which entered production in 1942, the year in which PzKpfw III production attained 2,600 machines. The PzKpfw III Ausf L was similar to the late-production Ausf J with the L/60 main gun in every external respect but armour, which now included a 0.79in (20mm) layer, 100mm (3.94in) above the superstructure and mantlet. This further increased the nose heaviness already evident in the Ausf J and earlier models retrofitted with the L/60 gun, and a torsion bar compensator was added to the suspension as the coil springs used in addition to the torsion bars of the front road wheels were inadequate for the task. Weight was reduced slightly by the limitation to a maximum of seventy-eight 50mm rounds. The exigencies of the war, especially on the Eastern Front, are reflected in the fact that photographic records show the Ausf L with a wide assortment of field modifications designed to provide improved protection. Designed to detonate incoming hollow-charge warheads before the latter reached the critical focus distance from a vulnerable point, skirt armour was a firm favourite: large rectangular plates were attached to the hull sides, extending far enough downwards to protect the running gear and being sufficiently high to protect the hull/turret junction line, while curved plates were often added around the turret and over the mantlet as additional protection.

In 1942 the PzKpfw III Ausf M also appeared, this being a variant of the Ausf L optimised for mass production by the elimination of the hull vision ports and escape doors. Although the elimination of the hull escape doors might be thought a retrograde step, it should be remembered that these were generally inoperable when essential skirt armour was fitted; at the same time, this move allowed a redistribution of ammunition stowage, increasing 50mm rounds to ninety-eight at the expense of machine-gun rounds which fell in number rom 4,950 to 2,550. Other features of the Ausf M were a wading capability to a depth of 4ft 11in (1.5m), and a valve system to allow hot engine coolant to be passed to another tank with the same system. This system was introduced in response to conditions on the Eastern Front, and made it possible for the engine of one tank to warm up that of another as a means of facilitating start-up in cold conditions.

Production of the Ausf M continued into 1943, but in 1942 the first examples of the ultimate PzKpfw III variant had appeared. This was the PzKpfw III Ausf N, identical to the deep-wading Ausf M in all respects but armament. In July

1942, Hitler had ordered that the Ausf L should be fitted with the obsolescent 75mm (2.95in) KwK L/24 gun in place of its current 50mm weapon. The German leader's intention was to provide a support tank for heavier tanks such as the PzKpfw VI Tiger, and the designated weapon was the ordnance of early models of the PzKpfw IV, weighing 628lb (285kg) and able to fire a 14.9lb (6.75kg) APCBC projectile with a muzzle velocity of 1,263ft (385m) per second, sufficient to penetrate 1.61in (41mm) of armour at an angle of 30° at a range of 545yds (500m). But whereas the 50mm weapon was limited to HE and armour-piercing ammunition, the 75mm (2.95in) weapon could fire armour-piercing, HEAT, HE, Smoke and Case projectiles, of which 56 rounds were carried in addition to 3,450 machine-gun rounds. The same ordnance was used in the Ausf N, which had revised ammunition stowage for sixty-four 75mm (2.95in) rounds. Production amounted to 660 Ausf N tanks in the period from July 1942 to August 1943, the 213 vehicles built in 1943 being modified in production with definitive *Schurze* (aprons): this comprised 0.315in (8mm) skirts over the running gear and 5mm (0.2in) panels around the turret. Further protection was afforded by *Zimmerit* paste, of which a 220lb (100kg) coating provided protection against magnetically attached mines.

Total production of the PzKpfw III was 5,644, and the type's importance on the development of armoured warfare cannot be exaggerated as it was the primary weapon of the Panzer divisions in their days of triumph between 1939 and 1941: the PzKpfw III led the Panzer divisions as they swept through Poland in 1939, the Low Countries and France in 1940, and the Balkans, North Africa and the USSR in 1941. For the first time in armoured warfare there was a mass-production battle tank design that could be upgunned without undue difficulty, and the type's combat record speaks for itself in terms of the results that were secured. The lesson was absorbed to the fullest extent by the Americans and the British, who hitherto had not considered armoured fighting vehicles as mass-production vehicles; in consequence, far greater thought was given to the longer-term production values that allowed the introduction of improved variants with heavier armament. The PzKpfw III also validated the concept of a common chassis for multiple applications, and of the 15,000 or so chassis produced, nearly 9,500 were used as the automotive/structural basis of vehicles other than tanks.

Panzerkampfwagen IV

Specification: PzKpfw IV Ausf D (4/BW) (SdKfz 161)

Country of origin: Germany

Type: Battlefield support tank

Crew: Five

Combat weight: 44,092lb (20,000kg)

Dimensions: Length overall 19ft 4.75in (5.91m); width 8ft 7in (2.92m) over steps; height overall 8ft 6in (2.59m)

Armament system: One 75mm (2.95in) KwK L/24 rifled gun with 80 rounds and two 7.92mm (0.312in) MG 34 machine-guns (one co-axial and one bow) with 2,800 rounds; the turret was electrically operated, the main gun was stabilised in neither elevation (unspecified elevation arc) nor azimuth (360°), and simple optical sights were fitted

Armour: Welded steel varying in thickness between 0.39 and 1.18in (10 and 30mm)

Powerplant: One 300hp (224kW) Maybach HL 120 PRM petrol engine with 103.4 Imp gal (470 litres) of fuel

Performance: Speed, road 26.1mph (42km/h); range, road 124 miles (200km); fording 2ft 7.5in (0.8m); gradient 57%; vertical obstacle 1ft 11.5in (0.6m); trench 7ft 6.5in (2.3m); ground clearance 15.75in (0.4m)

The last of Germany's main tanks with a pre-war pedigree was the PzKpfw IV, which also possesses the distinction of being the only German tank to have remained in production throughout World War II for an overall total of more than 8,500 examples. The type was planned at the same time as the PzKpfw III, and was essentially similar other than in its main armament, which was the 75mm (2.95in) KwK L/24 designed to provide the lighter PzKpfw III with HE fire support. The ordnance weighed 628lb (285kg) compared with the 37mm KwK L/45's 430lb (195kg) and the 50mm KwK L/42's 496lb (225kg): it fired its 14.9lb (6.75kg) APCBC projectile with a muzzle velocity of 1,263ft (385m) per second, sufficient to penetrate 1.61in (41mm) of armour at an angle of 30° at a range of 545yds (500m). In addition to this armour-piercing round, the KwK L/24 ordnance could fire HEAT, HE, Smoke and Case rounds. The standard tank battalion had four companies, and it was planned that while three of these would field the PzKpfw III battle tank, the fourth would operate the PzKpfw IV medium tank in the support role.

The design was fixed at a weight not exceeding 24 tonnes, and in 1934 prototype vehicles were ordered under the cover designation BW from Krupp as the VK2001(K), from MAN as the VK2002(MAN), and from Rheinmetall as the VK2001(Rh). The Krupp submission had large-diameter interleaved road wheels, and this was considered the best basis for a production tank, though only after incorporation of features from the Rheinmetall prototype, including the simpler running gear consisting on each side of eight small road wheels in two-wheel bogies with leaf springs; the drive sprocket was at the front and the idler at the rear, and there were four track-return rollers. In 1936, production contracts were let to Krupp for a vehicle to be designated PzKpfw IV (SdKfz 161), and in overall configuration similar to the PzKpfw III. The crew was disposed in much the same way as in the PzKpfw III, but whereas the battle tank had a manually operated turret, that of the medium tank was traversed electrically. Before the PzKpfw IV entered large-scale production, a number of features were trialled in small pre-production batches, of which the first was the PzKpfw IV Ausf A built to the extent of 35 examples. This weighed 38,139lb (17,300kg), was armoured from a minimum of 0.315in (8mm) to a maximum of 0.79in (20mm), and was armed with the 75mm (2.95in) main gun plus a secondary battery of two 7.92mm (0.312in) MG 34 machine-guns (one in the bow and the other co-axial). The Ausf A was powered by a 250hp (186kW) Maybach HL 108 TR petrol engine for a maximum speed of 18.6mph (30km/h), and its features included the distinctive air inlets on the rear decking and the commander's cupola projecting vertically through the rear of the angular but well-shaped turret.

Next came the PzKpfw IV Ausf B of 1938 with a modified cupola, a straight-fronted rather than recessed superstructure, no bow machine-gun, a 320hp (239kW) engine and a number of detail modifications; production amounted to 42 machines. The Ausf B formed the basis for the PzKpfw IV Ausf C, which followed in 1939 with a 300hp (224kW) engine, an armoured sleeve for the turret machine-gun, and armour increased in maximum thickness to 1.18in (30mm), so increasing weight from the 39,021lb (17,700kg) of the Ausf B to 44,092lb (20,000kg).

Full-scale production began late in 1939 with the PzKpfw IV Ausf D, which was based on the Ausf C but restored the bow machine-gun and introduced a stepped front to the superstructure. Other changes included an increase in the armour thickness of the glacis plate, hull sides and hull rear from 0.57 to 0.79in (14.5 to 20mm), an external rather than internal gun mantlet of 1.18in (30mm) thickness, eyelid shutters over the five vision ports in the commander's cupola, a new pattern of track, and slightly larger overall dimensions. The uparmouring of the Ausf D indicated that the German army was now becoming seriously worried about the comparatively thin armour of its primary tanks, and this process was continued with the PzKpfw IV Ausf E that was identical to the Ausf D in all but its improved protection and its new turret. The protective features included the thickening of the nose plate from 1.18 to 1.97in (30 to 50mm), but although it had been planned to increase the front plate to the same thickness, the design of the bow machine-gun installation precluded this until a new mounting had been designed. Increased protection was afforded to the fighting compartment by the addition of 0.79in (20mm) face-hardened armour plate on the sides, and in service the tank was often provided with additional protection by the addition of spaced armour of various types: this generally comprised 1.18in (30mm) panels attached over a 2.95in (75mm) gap to reduce the effect of hollow-charge warheads.

The Ausf E introduced the type of turret that remained standard on production vehicles for the rest of World War II. Some criticism had been levelled at the inadequate protection offered by the 0.79in (20mm) thickness of the commander's cupola, and in the revised turret this was increased to a minimum of 1.18in (30mm) and a maximum of 2.64in (67mm). The cupola was also moved forward, allowing the installation of a smoothly curved back plate without the distinctive cut-out previously necessary to accommodate the rear of the cupola. Finally, the turret was fitted with an electrical ventilation fan to provide better fighting conditions than had prevailed with the original ventilator flap.

While the PzKpfw III had been designed as the spearhead tank of the Panzer divisions, the PzKpfw IV had been schemed as the support weapon that could deal with heavier obstacles: but as the tide of the war began to sway against Germany, the limitations of the PzKpfw III's armament became clear: whereas the original concept of reliance upon a 37mm main gun (but allowing for subsequent revision to a 50mm weapon) had seemed sufficient in the mid-1930s, the situation in 1942 revealed without doubt that the original concept should have called for a 50mm gun with subsequent revision to a 75mm (2.95in) weapon. By 1942, therefore, the Allies were fielding substantial numbers of tanks with armour generally impervious to 50mm projectiles at all but the shortest ranges.

The first definitive variant of the PzKpfw IV was the PzKpfw Ausf F, its importance compared with the earlier SdKfz 161 variants exemplified by the allocation of a revised inventory designation, SdKfz 161/1. Although modelled on the preceding Ausf E, this variant was planned with thicker armour and a longer-barrelled 75mm (2.95in) main gun. The armour was to a 1.97in (50mm) basis rather than a 1.18in (30mm) basis, with maxima of 2.36 and 1.97in (60 and 50mm) on the hull and turret respectively, but the longer ordnance was not ready in time, and the standard KwK L/24 gun had to be fitted. The variant was built throughout 1941, and weighed 49,162lb (22,300kg). When the superior KwK 40 L/43 gun became available, it was introduced on an Ausf F variant known as the PzKpfw IV Ausf F2, earlier models being redesignated PzKpfw IV Ausf F1 retrospectively. The Ausf F2 weighed 52,028lb (23,600kg), and its advent marked an apex in German tank capability. The L/43 ordnance weighed 1,041lb (472kg), and fired its 15lb (6.8kg) armour-piercing projectile with a muzzle velocity of 2,428ft (740m) per second: this provided the projectile with the power to penetrate 3.5in (89mm) of armour at an angle of 30° at a range of 545yds (500m), translating into just over twice the penetration capability of the L/24 weapon at the same range. During 1941-42, German gun power had fallen below the best provided in American and Soviet tanks, but the L/43 gun restored parity at a time crucial to the German war effort. The German army was more than thankful for the restoration of parity, but quite rightly demanded tank gun superiority in the standard 75mm (2.95in) calibre: Krupp therefore produced an L/48 version of the KwK 40, the additional five calibres of barrel length adding 53lb (24kg) in weight and 14.96in (380mm) in overall length. The L/48 weapon thus weighed 1,093lb (496kg) and was 153.5in (3.9m) long, but as projectile muzzle velocity was boosted to only 2,461ft (750m) per second, the armour penetration capability was increased by only 0.12in (3mm) to 3.62in (92mm) at standard angle and range. The PzKpfw IV was still considered a dual-role weapon with anti-tank and support roles, and this fact was reflected in the KwK 40's

The variants of the PzKpfw IV up to the Ausf F1 were armed with a short-barrelled 75mm (2.95in) gun suitable for the support task rather than the anti-tank role.

ammunition types, which included APCBC, APCR, HEAT, HE and Smoke.

The Ausf F2 was succeeded by the PzKpfw IV Ausf G, which was basically similar to its predecessor apart from detail modifications and improved armour, the latter including a thicker top to the superstructure. Field additions often included spaced frontal armour and *Schurze* of the types also used in the PzKpfw III's later variants, for protection against hollow-charge warheads carried by Allied weapons such as Soviet anti-tank grenades, American 'bazooka' rocket-launchers and British PIAT projectors. The L/48 version of the KwK 40 gun was introduced on the PzKpfw IV Ausf H version of this increasingly important tank, which received the revised inventory designation SdKfz 161/2 in recognition of its importance. The Ausf H began to leave the production lines in March 1943, and was similar to the Ausf F2 and Ausf G apart from its use of the longer gun, a revised turret hatch cover, cast rather than fabricated drive sprockets, improved frontal armour of the spaced type, and, as a measure of protection for the increasingly vulnerable flanks, 0.315in (8mm) turret and 0.2in (5mm) skirt armour. This resulted in an increase in combat weight to 55,115lb (25,000kg), but the retention of the same 300hp (224kW) engine inevitably caused a loss of performance signalised by a maximum speed of 23.6mph (38km/h).

By the beginning of 1943, the limitations of the PzKpfw III and PzKpfw IV were clear to field commanders and procurement authorities alike, and in February it was proposed that the PzKpfw IV should be supplanted in production by the new PzKpfw V Panther and PzKpfw VI Tiger tanks. In essence the notion was correct, but as men such as General Heinz Guderian were swift to point out, production rates of the newer vehicles were so low that the PzKpfw IV should be retained in order to maintain the numerical strength of the Panzer arm in the decisive year of 1943, which saw the strategic initiative swing firmly towards the Allied nations in events such as the German defeat at Stalingrad (February 1943), in North Africa (May 1943), at Kursk and in Sicily (July 1943), and at Salerno (September 1943). Hitler therefore decided that production of the PzKpfw IV should continue at least to the beginning of 1944, and this paved the way for the evolution of the final production variant, the PzKpfw IV Ausf J that began to reach combat units in March 1944.

The designers had taken the lessons of combat firmly to heart and produced a variant that was easier to manufacture and more effective in combat, yet lighter than its predecessors. The Ausf J had thicker frontal armour, including 3.15in (80mm) for the front plate, driver's plate and mantlet, combined with flank protection by wire mesh screens in place of the heavy skirts of the Ausf F, G and H variants. A revised exhaust system was incorporated, as well as a new transmission and provision for wading to a depth of 3ft 11.25in (1.2m). Earlier models had been provided with a power system plus manual back-up for turret traverse, but in the Ausf J the power traverse system was removed (and the manual system altered to a two-speed geared unit) to provide greater fuel capacity. The Ausf J was thus a more capable machine than the Ausf H, and remained in production right to the end of World War II, the total for the two models reaching almost 6,000 chassis (from a total of 9,000 PzKpfw IV tanks) in the last two years of the war.

The PzKpfw IV fought on every German front in World War II, and proved itself one of the most important tanks ever produced. Although it was always armed with a 75mm (2.95in) main gun, the adoption of longer-barrelled ordnances of this calibre allowed the designers to keep the tank current with most Western and many Soviet tanks, and when properly handled the PzKpfw IV was still a capable adversary. Like the PzKpfw III, the PzKpfw IV is also of significance for its well-proved chassis, which was adopted for many other tracked vehicles.

Panzerkampfwagen V Panther

Specification: PzKpfw Panther Ausf G (SdKfz 171)

Country of origin: Germany

Type: Battle tank

Crew: Five

Combat weight: 99,868lb (45,300kg)

Dimensions: Length, gun forward 29ft 0.75in (8.86m) andhull 22ft 9in (6.935m); width 10ft 8.75in (3.27m); height overall 9ft 10in (2.995m)

Armament system: One 75mm (2.95in) KwK 42 L/70 rifled gun with 79 rounds, two or three 7.92mm (0.3in) MG 34 machine-guns (one co-axial, one bow and one optional AA) with 4,500 rounds, and one 92mm (3.62in) Nahverteidigungswaffe bomb/grenade launcher; the turret was hydraulically operated, the main gun was stabilised in neither elevation (-4• to +20•) nor azimuth (360•), and simple optical sights were fitted

Armour: Welded steel varying in thickness between 0.51 and 4.72in (13 and 120mm)

Powerplant: One 700hp (522kW) Maybach HL 230 P30 petrol engine with 160.6 Imp gal (730 litres) of fuel

Performance: Speed, road 28.4mph (45.7km/h); range, road 124 miles (200km); fording 6ft 2.75in (1.9m); gradient 70%; vertical obstacle 2ft 11.5in (0.9m); trench 8ft 0.5in (2.45m); ground clearance 22in (0.56m)

On 20 November 1941 a German investigation team assessed a captured T-34 medium tank and came to the conclusion that the Soviet tank had significant advantages over German tanks in its sloped armour, its large road wheels and its long gun. The sloping of the armour offered an effective increase in thickness without the weight penalty of vertical protection of this actual thickness; the large road

wheels offered a superior ride, especially across country; and the long gun, hitherto rejected by the Germans as impractical for a number of reasons, offered very high muzzle velocity and therefore a devastating armour-penetration capability. The inevitable conclusion was that all current German tanks were obsolete in the technical sense, and an immediate programme was launched to produce a counter to the T-34: within five days the German armaments ministry contracted with Daimler-Benz and MAN for VK3002 designs to meet a specification that demanded a 30/35-tonne battle tank with a 75mm (2.95in) main gun, well-sloped armour to a maximum thickness of 1.57in (40mm) on the sides and 2.36in (60mm) on the front, and a maximum speed of 34.1mph (55km/h). In January 1942 the specification was revised to include a 37.3mph (60km/h) maximum speed and frontal armour of 2.36in (60mm) on the hull and 3.94in (100mm) on the turret.

The VK3002(DB) and VK3002(MAN) designs were completed in April 1942. The VK3002(DB) was essentially a

The PzKpfw V Panther was designed after the Germans had first encountered the Soviet T-34 medium tank and copied features such as the large road wheels (interleaved in this application and fitted with torsion-bar suspension), well-sloped armour, and a long-barrelled 75mm (2.95in) gun fitted with a double-baffle muzzle brake for a high muzzle velocity without overlong recoil travel.

German copy of the T-34, with the turret located so far forward that the driver sat inside the turret cage and had to use a hydraulically operated remote steering system. The gun mantlet was effectively a continuation of the glacis plate, the fighting compartment was large and uncluttered, and the Daimler-Benz MB 507 diesel engine was located in the rear compartment: the use of a diesel offered considerable advantages in terms of range, safety and availability of fuel. External but jettisonable fuel tanks were envisaged for the combination of range with safety, the drive sprockets were at the rear, and to ease production the interleaved road wheels were designed without rubber tyres and were fitted with leaf-spring rather than torsion bar suspension. Overall, the VK3002(DB) was a design of great potential, and an order for 200 was placed at the express instruction of Hitler, whose only demand was that the planned 75mm (2.95in) L/48 gun of Krupp design should be replaced by a Rheinmetall L/70 weapon of the same calibre. Prototype construction was started soon after the placement of the order, but was cancelled in the later months of 1942.

The armament ministry, on the other hand, preferred

the VK3002(MAN), which was powered by a proved petrol engine and, in the short term at least, was better suited to German production practices.

The VK3002(MAN) had a basic layout similar to that of the PzKpfw IV, with the driver and radio operator/bow machine-gunner in the forward compartment, the commander, gunner and loader in the fighting compartment that was located in the centre of the vehicle, and the Maybach HL 210 engine in the rear compartment but powering forward drive sprockets for the comparatively wide tracks, which ran over an assembly, on each side, of eight interleaved road wheels with torsion bar suspension. The new vehicle was considerably more powerful than earlier German tanks, having more than twice the horsepower of the PzKpfw IV, and a special gearbox was developed to allow optimum use of this potential for high speed and good cross-country performance. The rubber-tyred road wheels were of sufficiently large diameter to obviate the need for track-return rollers. The turret was located as far back as possible to reduce the type of mobility and tactical problems that might otherwise have been caused by a long barrel overhang of the L/60 gun originally planned for the vehicle: this problem would have been acute with the forward-mounted turret of the VK3002(DB), especially when the failure of the L/60 gun led to the adoption of the longer L/70 main armament; the armament specification called for an armour-penetration capability of 5.51in (140mm) at a range of 1,095yds (1,000m).

Mild-steel prototypes of the MAN design were ordered in May 1942, and such was the importance allocated to the programme that the army ministry's chief tank designer, Dipl. Ing. Kniepkampf, was seconded to MAN to supervise the whole project. The first prototype of the VK3002(MAN) appeared in September 1942. It was launched on a large-scale evaluation programme, and because of the gravity of Germany's armour position on the Eastern Front (compounded by technical problems with the new PzKpfw VI Tiger heavy tank), the type was ordered into immediate production as the PzKpfw V Panther (SdKfz 171). The first production Panther appeared in November 1942, and although production was envisaged at the rate of 250 vehicles per month, this already ambitious figure was almost immediately raised to 600 per month. This figure was never achieved, despite the launch of a large-scale co-production system involving four major manufacturers, and the 1944 monthly average was 330, leading to an overall total of 5,590 Panthers by the end of World War II, including 1,850 in the first year of production and 3,740 between January 1944 and May 1945. An additional 679 chassis were completed for use in roles such as recovery (the Bergepanzer Panther, or Bergepanther), command (Befehlspanzer Panther), artillery observation (Beobachtungspanzer Panther) and tank destroying (Panzerjäger Panther, or Jagdpanther).

The German army's maximum weight limit of 35 tonnes had proved impossible to meet, and the Panther turned the scales at a weight of 100,309lb (45,500kg) from its service debut. This weight was attributable mostly to Hitler's insistence on thicker armour, and, as a result, plans were laid for use of the bored-out HL 230 in place of the originally specified HL 210 engine: even so, the reduced maximum speed of 28mph (45km/h) had to be accepted.

The first 20 Panthers were designated PzKpfw V Panther Ausf A, and were essentially pre-production machines with 2.36in (60mm) frontal armour as demanded by the original specification, a 642hp (479kW) HL 210 engine, a ZF-7 rather than the definitive AK 7-200 gearbox, an early model of the L/70 main gun, and the commander's cupola at the extreme left of the Rheinmetall turret. Considerable development work was undertaken with these first Panthers, which were redesignated PzKpfw V Panther Ausf D1 early in 1943. The proposed second and third production models were the Ausf B with a Maybach Olvar gearbox, and the Ausf C of which no details have been found. Trials with the Ausf A revealed a number of problems, but the importance of the programme was such that no delay in the overall production programme was authorised to allow a full examination and rectification of the deficiencies before they were built into service tanks. The problems stemmed mostly from the rushed development of the Panther, which was considerably heavier and more powerful than first planned, and without significant modification of the gearbox, cooling system and running gear. The most important of these problems were failures in the bolts attaching the rubber tyres to the road wheels (entailing the removal of up to five complete wheels when an inner wheel failed), failure of the final drive gears (often causing transmission gear, differential and steering failures), and engine overheating.

The first real production variant was therefore the PzKpfw V Panther Ausf D, which was redesignated PzKpfw V

Panther Ausf D2 at the same time that the Ausf A became the Ausf D1. The type appeared in January 1943, and featured the standard type of 'dustbin' cupola, a vision port and a machine-gun port in the glacis plate, the definitive L/70 main gun with a double-baffle muzzle brake to reduce recoil distance in an already cramped turret, smoke-dischargers on each side of the turret and, on later production examples, skirt armour added during construction, together with a coating of *Zimmerit* anti-mine paste; these later vehicles also had a grenade-launcher above the turret, in place of the flanking smoke-dischargers.

The next variant appeared in July 1943, and should have been the Ausf E, but for reasons which remain unexplained was in fact designated the PzKpfw V Panther Ausf A. This incorporated features that had been omitted during production of the Ausf D2, in order to hasten preparation for the Germans' final effort in July 1943 to regain the strategic initiative on the Eastern Front in the Battle of Kursk, which was the world's largest-ever tank battle. Kursk was the Panther's combat debut, most available vehicles serving with one army and three SS divisions of the 4th Panzerarmee: the Panthers were more than a match for the Soviet T-34s, but they seldom ran for more than a few miles without a mechanical problem. The Panthers had been rushed into service so quickly that there was no adequate recovery vehicle, and as many as three large half-tracks were required to extricate a broken-down Panther. Hitler's insistence on use of the Panthers at Kursk was a profound error forced on a reluctant army: used in small numbers, by crews inexperienced with the type and therefore unable to overcome the type's lack of mechanical maturity, the Panthers had little tactical impact but were revealed prematurely as the potent weapons they were to become, allowing the Soviets to develop counter-tactics in good time.

The Ausf A introduced the definitive commander's cupola with better ballistic shaping and armoured periscopes, a fully-engineered ball mounting for the hull machine-gun, a monocular rather than binocular gunner's sight in the turret, and elimination of all turret pistol spent-case ejection ports.

The final production variant of the original Panther series was designated PzKpfw Panther Ausf G, reflecting Hitler's order for the roman numeral in the original designation to be omitted. The origins of this model lay with the February 1942 instruction of the German armaments ministry that

MAN was to co-operate with Henschel in the development of a Panther variant that incorporated as many PzKpfw VI Tiger components as possible. The programme would have resulted in the Panther II Ausf F with the interleaved steel wheels of the Tiger II, thicker armour on the hull top, a turret modelled on that of the Tiger Ausf B with stereoscopic rangefinder and gun stabilisation system, the higher-rated AK 7-400 gearbox, and greater power in the form of the HL 230 rated to 800hp (596kW) with petrol injection and a higher compression ratio, and to 900hp (671kW) with a supercharger. The *Panzerturm schmal* (small tank turret) was designed by Daimler-Benz to accommodate L/70 or even L/100 versions of the KwK 42, or the 88mm (3.46in) KwK 43 L/71 gun as used in the Tiger II.

The Panther II would have entered production in the summer of 1945, and would probably have been a truly devastating weapon had the war continued into the autumn and winter of that year: its only feature to appear in the interim Panther Ausf G was the Tiger's resilient steel wheel, which finally removed the Panther's long-term problem with shed tyres. Other modifications included revised and thicker hull sides inclined at a greater angle, a modified mantlet of simpler construction, elimination of the driver's vision port, revised stowage arrangements (including main ammunition capacity increased from seventy-nine to eighty-two rounds), and better attachments for the skirt armour.

The most famous of the Panther's variants was the Jagdpanther, more formally known as the Panzerjäger Panther (SdKfz 173), a potent tank destroyer with the classic 88mm (3.46in) PaK 43/3 anti-tank gun mounted in a limited-traverse mounting in the forward face of the fixed superstructure.

It is hard to overestimate the importance of the Panther to armoured warfare in World War II or to the development of the tank since that time. An indication of the Panther's capabilities is attested by the fact that its frontal armour was impenetrable to the projectiles of the Allies' main gun tanks, while its own manoeuvrability and gun power allowed it to knock out the Allied tanks from stand-off range. One American estimate suggests that one Panther required the attentions of at least five M4 Sherman tanks if it was to be killed in a stalking engagement, resulting in a decisive flank or rear shot by one of the US tanks; otherwise, the Allies' best course of action was to try for a mobility kill, halting the tank with a blow to its trackwork.

Panzerkampfwagen VI **T**iger

Specification: PzKpfw Tiger Ausf E (SdKfz 181)

Country of origin: Germany

Type: Heavy battle tank

Crew: Five

Combat weight: 125,441lb (56,900kg)

Dimensions: Length, gun forward 27ft 9in (8.46m) and hull 20ft 8.75in (6.32m); width 12ft 2.75in (3.73m); height overall 9ft 6in (2.9m)

Armament system: One 88mm (3.46in) KwK 36 L/56 rifled gun with 92 rounds, two or three 7.92mm (0.312in) MG 34 machine-guns (one co-axial, one bow and one optional AA) with 5,100 rounds, and three smoke-dischargers on each side of the turret or one 92mm (3.62in) Nahverteidigungswaffe bomb/grenade launcher; the turret was hydraulically operated, the main gun was stabilised in neither elevation (-6.5° to +17°) nor azimuth (360°), and optical sights were fitted

Armour: Welded steel varying in thickness between 1.02 and 4.33in (26 and 110mm)

Powerplant: One 642hp (478.7kW) Maybach HL 210 P45 (first 250 vehicles) or 694hp (517.4kW) Maybach HL 230 P45 petrol engine with 124.7 Imp gal (567 litres) of fuel

Performance: Speed, road 23mph (37km/h); range, road 72.7 miles (117km); fording 4ft 0in (1.22m) without preparation or 13ft 1.5in (4.0m) with snorkel; gradient 70%; vertical obstacle 2ft 7in (0.79m); trench 7ft 6.5in (2.3m); ground clearance 16.9in (0.43m)

The largest German tanks to see combat in World War II were the variants of the PzKpfw VI Tiger series which, despite its higher numerical designator, in fact appeared before the PzKpfw V Panther. In 1937 the German army appreciated the high qualities of its new PzKpfw III battle tanks and PzKpfw IV medium tanks, but also realised that a heavier tank might form a useful adjunct in the assault role. In that year, therefore, Henschel received an order for two prototypes of a 30/33-tonne heavy tank designated DW.I (the prefix standing for *Durchbruchswagen*, or break-through vehicle). The design emerged as a massive machine with interleaved road wheels, and testing of the first prototype hull was in progress when Henschel was instructed to drop the concept and devote its energies instead to a truly huge design, the VK6501. This was to be a 65-tonne machine armed with a 75mm (2.95in) main gun plus a secondary armament of machine-guns in separate turrets: evolved conceptually and mechanically from the PzKpfw NbFz (PzKpfw V), the VK6501 was planned for production as the PzKpfw VII but was cancelled in 1940, even as the two prototype chassis were being tested. The emphasis now returned to a heavy tank derived from the DW.I, which Henschel had refined into the DW.2 with a weight of 70,547lb (32,000kg), a crew of five, and an armament of one

Thickly protected, and powerfully armed with an 88mm (3.46in) gun, the PzKpfw VI Tiger was also extremely heavy. The power-to-weight ratio was low, however, and this meant that the Tiger was slow and lacked manoeuvrability.

short-barrel 75mm (2.95in) gun and two 7.92mm (0.312in) machine-guns. Trials with the DW.2 continued into 1941, but more definitive plans had already matured within the German official hierarchy to make the DW.2 obsolete as a contender for production orders. These plans called for a 30-tonne breakthrough tank armed with a 75mm (2.95in) main gun, and after design proposals had been solicited from Daimler-Benz, Henschel, MAN and Porsche, orders were placed with Henschel and Porsche for eight prototypes (four from each company): the Henschel machine was the VK3001(H) and the Porsche machine the VK3001(P).

The VK3001(H) was a logical development from the DW.2, and the four prototypes appeared as two in March 1941 and two in October 1941, differing from each other only in detail. The superstructure was similar to that of the PzKpfw IV, and the running gear, on each side, comprised seven interleaved road wheels with three track-return rollers. The armament was the 75mm (2.95in) KwK 40 L/48 gun, but as the prototypes were being evaluated, the T-34 made its appearance on the Eastern Front and at a stroke rendered obsolete any German plans for a new tank with the 75mm (2.95in) gun that was patently inferior to the 76.2mm (3in) weapon of the Soviet tank. Whereas the VK3001(H) was completely orthodox in its concept and mechanical features, the same cannot be said of the VK3001(P) from the innovative Dr Ferdinand Porsche, who called his creation the Typ 100 Leopard. This resembled the VK3001(H) in overall design, but its running gear, on each side, comprised six road wheels and two track-return rollers, the suspension was of the longitudinal rather than transverse torsion bar type, and power was provided by a novel petrol-electric drive system. Daimler-Benz and MAN also produced prototypes, but these are believed not to have progressed as far as the Henschel and Porsche types, which were in fact never fitted with their turrets. The VK3001 concept was shown to be obsolete by the advent of the T-34, and the Germans sensibly cancelled further work on the prototypes.

The Germans had been working concurrently on a heavier tank concept largely to satisfy the demands of Hitler, who was developing into a firm advocate of heavy tanks with powerful armament and protection. The German leader had been impressed by aspects of the technical reports about the British and French infantry-support tanks encountered by the German forces in the Western campaign of May and June 1940, and especially the extent of their armour protection. This had proved invulnerable to the German tank guns of the period, and Hitler now sought to provide the German forces with tanks providing a comparable level of protection with decisively heavier firepower and adequate mobility. For firepower, Hitler's demand was a weapon capable of penetrating 3.94in (100mm) of armour at a range of 1,640yds (1,500m), and in line with the standard German practice of the time, the tank was to be protected against a comparable weapon. The German leader's first choice for the main gun was a tank development of the 88mm (3.46in) FlaK 36 dual-role anti-aircraft and anti-tank gun, while the German ordnance department preferred a smaller-calibre weapon using the tapered-bore concept of barrel and ammunition design to provide the same armour-penetration capability: the use of a 60 or 75mm (2.36 or 2.95in) weapon, the department argued, would allow stowage of a larger number of rounds in any given volume, and would also allow a reduction in tank size and weight with consequent advantages in cost and performance.

It was decided to produce a 36-tonne prototype with the tapered-bore gun and the designation VK3601(H). But the tapered-bore gun required considerable quantities of increasingly scarce tungsten, and was cancelled by Hitler at about the time the VK3001 and VK3601 concepts were halted in favour of a larger 45-tonne tank, ordered in the form of competing VK4501(H) and VK4501(P) prototypes in May 1941. The contracts stipulated that the prototypes should be ready for Hitler's birthday on 20 April 1942: each type was to use a Krupp-designed turret accommodating the 88mm (3.46in) KwK 36 L/56 gun. Henschel used features of its VK3001 and VK3601 prototypes in the VK3601(H), which was proposed as the VK3601(H1) with the Krupp turret and an 88mm (3.46in) gun, and as the VK3601(H2) with a Rheinmetall turret and a 75mm (2.95in) KwK 42 L/70 gun. The H2 variant was never built and the first prototypes of the VK3601(H1) variant appeared in March 1942. The tank was modelled on the VK3001, although the road wheels were of larger diameter, thereby removing the need for track-return rollers.

The VK4501(P) appeared in the following month, and was modelled on the VK3001(P) with the same type of petrol-electric drive and longitudinal torsion bar suspension. Comparative trials confirmed the overall

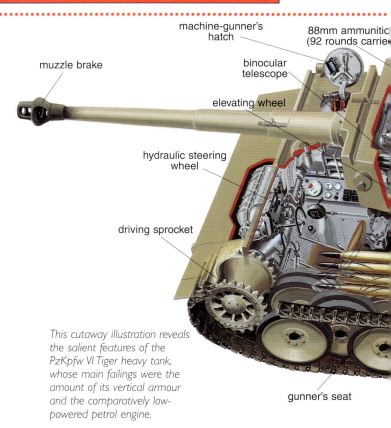

machine-gunner's hatch

88mm ammunitic (92 rounds carrie

muzzle brake

binocular telescope

elevating wheel

hydraulic steering wheel

driving sprocket

This cutaway illustration reveals the salient features of the PzKpfw VI Tiger heavy tank, whose main failings were the amount of its vertical armour and the comparatively low-powered petrol engine.

gunner's seat

superiority of the VH4501(H), although it was as much as 24,250lb (11,000kg) over legend weight, and in August 1942 the type was ordered into production under the designation PzKpfw VI Tiger Ausf H (SdKfz 181) with the KwK 36 gun. This weighed 2,932lb (1,330kg), and its L/56 barrel provided for a muzzle velocity of 2,657ft (810m) per second, sufficient to give the 20.72lb (9.4kg) APCBC projectile the ability to penetrate 4.4in (112mm) of armour at an angle of 30° at a range of 545yds (500m). Combined with stowage for 92 rounds, this provided the Tiger with an anti-tank capability unmatched anywhere in the world at that time.

A back-up order was placed for 90 examples of the Porsche design as the PzKpfw VI VK4501(P) Tiger (P) in case the Henschel type should encounter problems, but when it became clear that the Henschel Tiger was proceeding without difficulty, these Porsche chassis were modified during construction into tank destroyers with the designation Panzerjäger Tiger (P) Ferdinand (SdKfz

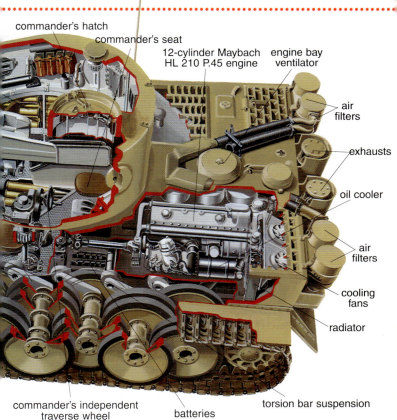

commander's hatch

commander's seat

12-cylinder Maybach HL 210 P.45 engine

engine bay ventilator

air filters

exhausts

oil cooler

air filters

cooling fans

radiator

commander's independent traverse wheel

batteries

torsion bar suspension

184), though the name was subsequently changed to Elefant.

Production of the Tiger lasted from August 1942 to August 1944, and totalled 1,350 vehicles. Production peaked in April 1944, when 104 vehicles were delivered: the original rate planned by the armaments ministry had been 12 vehicles per month, but at Hitler's insistence this had been increased to 25 vehicles per month by November 1942, increasing as the type proved itself in combat. In February 1944 the designation was revised, and the vehicle then became the PzKpfw Tiger Ausf E (SdKfz 181), this change being contemporary with a modification of the production standard to include a new cupola, simplified fittings, and resilient steel wheels in place of the original type with rubber tyres.

The Tiger was a massive machine, and its design epitomises the design of the classic 'German tank' of World War II: this was evolved before the T-34 hammered home the advantages of sloped armour (as copied by the Germans in the Panther), and the Tiger was thus the next in logical sequence from the PzKpfw IV with basically upright armour. In so large and heavy a machine the designers were faced with acute problems of hull rigidity, especially against the torsional effect of recoil when the gun was fired at any angle off the centreline. For this reason, the basic structure made use of the largest possible one-piece plates: the 1.02in (26mm) belly plate, for example, was a single piece some 5ft 11in (1.8m) wide and 15ft 11in (4.85m) long, and the interlocking armour plates were all welded. The curved sides and rear of the turret were made of a single piece of armour 3.15in (80mm) thick, bent into a horseshoe shape and connected across the front by a 3.94in (100mm) front plate whose opening for the gun was protected by a 4.33in (110mm) mantlet. The whole impression conveyed by the vehicle was of angular strength, and this impression is confirmed in reality by the armour inclination (at the most, 24° from the vertical) and thickness varying from 1.02in (26mm) on the belly and hull roof via 2.36in (60mm) on the lower sides, and 3.23in (82mm) on the upper sides and rear, to 3.94in (100mm) on the nose and front plate. This gives a good indication of how a combat weight of 121,252lb (55,000kg) or more was reached.

The movement of this mass required considerable power: the first 250 vehicles had the 642hp (479kW) Maybach HL 210 P45 petrol engine, and the rest had the 694hp (517.5kW) HL 230 P45 from the same manufacturer. The engine drove the forward drive sprockets via the coupled preselector gearbox/regenerative steering system, and on each side the running gear comprised eight large-diameter road wheels, with the idler to their rear. These were the first interleaved road wheels used on a German service tank, and provided an admirable ride: their main fault appeared in the winter, when slush and mud caught between the wheels tended to freeze overnight and thus immobilise the tank. The driver and bow machine-gunner/radio operator were located in the forward compartment, the commander, gunner and loader in the centrally-located fighting compartment, and the engine in the rear compartment. Tactical limitations with the Tiger included the use of hydraulic power from an engine-driven motor for turret traverse, necessitating the heavy turret to be moved in secondary manual mode when the engine was shut down, and the prodigious thirst of the engine, which consumed the maximum 125 Imp gal (570 litres) of petrol in only 74 miles (120km) on roads, or 43.5 miles (70km) across country. This short range was an added inducement to use the Tiger as an ambush tank rather than a mobile warfare tank, and the high points of its career were thus in the close-country campaigns such as those waged in Normandy (June and July 1944) and the Ardennes (December 1944).

Impressed with the offensive potential of the new vehicle, Hitler overruled his army commanders and demanded that the Tiger should be rushed into action as soon as possible. Given its weight and high ground-pressure even on its wide 28.15in (715mm) combat tracks, the Tiger was best suited to operations on firm ground, offering the possibility of ambush positions where the Tiger's powerful protection and devastating armament would give it a marked tactical advantage over numerically superior Allied types. In fact, the Tiger was first committed in unsuitable terrain outside Leningrad in September 1942, and suffered a high proportion of losses to the Soviets' carefully sited and extremely potent anti-tank defences. The Tigers were organised in 30-strong battalions, at first under command of corps or army headquarters; it was later planned to provide all Panzer divisions with an organic Tiger battalion, but only the more favoured of SS Panzer divisions actually received such a battalion.

The only three Tiger variants were the Panzerbefehlswagen Tiger Ausf E command tank, which was produced in SdKfz 267 and SdKfz 268 variants with additional radio equipment, the Bergepanzer Tiger Ausf E (SdKfz 185) recovery vehicle, and the Sturmtiger assault weapon with a 14.96in (380mm) mortar in a fixed superstructure.

At about the time that the Tiger entered production, the Germans decided to develop a new model with better armament and protection in case the Soviets produced another surprise after the T-34. Again, Henschel and Porsche were asked to develop competing designs with sloped armour and the new 88mm (3.46in) KwK 43 gun. This weapon was considerably heavier and longer than the KwK 36, and at a weight of 3,726lb (1,690kg) and a length of 263in (6.68m) compared with 209.45in (5.32m), but its L/71 barrel provided for a muzzle velocity of 3,346ft (1,020m) per second for the ability to penetrate 7.17in (182mm) of armour at an angle of 30° at a range of 545yds (500m) with its 22.49lb (10.2kg) APCBC projectile.

Otherwise known as the Königstiger (King tiger), the PzKpfw VI Tiger II was a much improved development of the Tiger I, and possessed much in common with the Panther in its better sloped armour. The type was very heavy, however, and this proved a severe tactical limitation for the comparatively few vehicles that were completed before Germany's defeat in May 1945.

Porsche responded with the VK4502(P), based on the VK4501(P) but carrying a beautifully shaped turret offering excellent ballistic protection and at first intended for a 150mm (5.91in) L/37 or 105mm (4.13in) L/70 gun, but then revised (in line with the army's thinking of the period) to an 88mm (3.46in) L/71 gun. The VK4502(P) was thought the likely winner by Porsche, who organised the casting process for the turret before the receipt of any production order: but whereas the petrol-electric drive of the VK4501(P) had been rejected largely for its novelty, the basically similar system of the VK4502(P) was now rejected because the copper required for its electric motors was now in very short supply.

The winning design was therefore Henschel's VK4503(H), although the first 50 production vehicles were fitted with the Porsche turret before the comparable Henschel type became standard: the Porsche turret was recognisable by the cut-away lower edge of the turret front, creating a dangerous shot trap between the gun and the roof of the hull; the Henschel turret had a straight front dropping right down to the hull roof without the Porsche turret's dangerous re-entrant. The Henschel design had been completed later than anticipated, the delay to October 1943 being attributable mainly to the armament ministry's desire to standardise as many parts as possible between the new tank and the planned Panther II. Henschel thereby lost

a considerable amount of time in liaison with MAN. Production finally began in December 1943 alongside the Tiger (now sometimes known as the Tiger I to differentiate it from its more powerful companion), and the type began to enter service in the spring of 1944, and first saw action on the Eastern Front in May 1944. Production continued to the end of World War II and amounted to 485 vehicles, known to the Allies as the Royal Tiger or King Tiger, to the German soldiers as the Königstiger (King Tiger) and to German officialdom as the PzKpfw VI Tiger II Ausf B (SdKfz 182), revised at about the time of the tank's introduction to PzKpfw Tiger II Ausf B (SdKfz 182).

To a certain extent, the Tiger II should be regarded as the heavyweight counterpart to the Panther rather than as a successor to the Tiger, and certainly the Tiger II had similarities to the Panther in its configuration, sloped armour and similar powerplant. This comprised a 694hp (517kW) Maybach HL 230 P30 petrol engine for a 153,660lb (69,700kg) vehicle, considerably heavier than the Panther at 100,309lb (45,500kg) and the Tiger I at 121,252lb (55,000kg). The results were inevitable: reduced performance and agility as the power-to-weight ratio was poorer than that of both the Panther and the Tiger, unreliability as the engine and transmission were overstressed, and a dismal maximum range of 68 miles (110km). These failings were perhaps excusable in a tank now used for defensive warfare, its sole offensive outing being the 'Battle of the Bulge' of December 1944, when many Tiger IIs broke down or ran out of fuel and were abandoned by their crews.

On the credit side, however, the Tiger II was the heaviest and therefore the best-armed and best-protected tank of World War II. The construction of the vehicle was of welded and well-sloped armour varying in thickness from a minimum of 0.98in (25mm) on the belly to a maximum of 5.91in (150mm) on the hull upper front; the turret was also welded of armour up to 3.94in (100mm) thick. The internal layout was standard, with the driver and bow machine-gunner/radio operator in the forward compartment, the commander, gunner and loader in the central fighting compartment, and the engine plus associated transmission in the rear compartment. As in the Tiger I, the massive turret was hydraulically powered from the engine, with manual operation for back-up and for those occasions when the engine was shut down.

The only Tiger II variant was the very powerful Panzerjäger Tiger Ausf B, a tank destroyer with armour to a maximum thickness of 9.84in (250mm) and a fixed superstructure accommodating a 128mm (5.04in) PaK 44 L/55 high-velocity gun firing a 62.4lb (28.3kg) armour-piercing projectile. This vehicle weighed 158,069lb (71,700kg) but retained the standard HL 230 P30 engine, resulting in yet further problems of reliability and mobility. Only a few were placed in service, but these proved truly formidable weapons when they had fuel and worked properly. Fuel was a constant problem for the Germans in the last year of the war, and the problem became decisively acute in the five months of war during 1945. Germany's massive tanks of the Panther and Tiger series were good vehicles, using their firepower and protection to counter the Allies' numerical superiority in armoured vehicles of all types, but were finally immobilised for want of fuel. The significance of these operational tanks is proved by the interest with which captured examples were examined by the victorious Western Allies, their many good features being assessed for incorporation into the new generation of post-war tanks demanded by the Americans and the British.

T-34

Specification: T-34/76B

Country of origin: USSR

Type: Medium tank

Crew: Four

Combat weight: 62,280lb (28,250kg)

Dimensions: Length, gun forward 21ft 7in (6.58m) and hull 19ft 11in (6.07m); width 9ft 10in (3.0m); height overall 8ft 0.5in (2.45m)

Armament system: One 76.2mm (3in) M1938 L-11 L/41.2 rifled gun with 77 rounds and two 7.62mm (0.3in) DT machine-guns (one co-axial and one bow) with 3,000 rounds; the turret was electrically operated, the main gun was stabilised in neither elevation (-3° to +30°) nor azimuth (360°), and optical sights were fitted; smoke could be generated by injecting diesel fuel into the exhaust

Armour: Welded steel varying in thickness between 0.79 and 2.56in (20 and 65mm)

Powerplant: One 500hp (373kW) V-2-34 diesel engine with 135.3 Imp gal (615 litres) of fuel

Performance: Speed, road 32mph (51.5km/h); range, road 280 miles (450km); fording 4ft 6in (1.37m); gradient 70%; vertical obstacle 2ft 4in (0.71m); trench 9ft 10in (3.0m); ground clearance 16.1in (0.41m)

The T-34 was, without doubt, the most important tank of World War II, and arguably the most influential tank ever developed. By Western standards the tank was mechanically unsophisticated, with its four-speed gearbox and clutch/brake steering, but the power train and running gear/suspension were ruthlessly reliable, the armament formidable and the protection far superior to that of the German PzKpfw IV tank. Small-scale encounters with T-34 units began to be recorded by the Germans as early as June 1941, but fully operational T-34 units were encountered with increasing frequency in the autumn of the same year. The advent of the T-34 was an enormous and thoroughly unpleasant surprise to the Germans, for up to this point in World War II their Panzer divisions had enjoyed an unequalled blend of tactical superiority and technical advantage; from this moment the Germans' technical edge was gone, and their tactical expertise was gradually matched even if never excelled by the Soviets.

The origins of the T-34 are evolutionary, lying firmly with the BT series of fast tanks using the Christie running gear/-suspension. The main development centre for the BT series was Kharkov, and in 1936 the brilliant designer M.I. Koshkin was sent to the Komintern plant to continue development of the BT series with the assistance of A.A. Morozov, N.A. Kucherenko and M.I. Tarshinov. The first result of Koshkin's labours was the A-20 medium tank that appeared at the beginning of 1938. This was modelled on the BT-IS and weighed 44,092lb (20,000kg). The armament was the medium-calibre 45mm L/46 gun, which weighed 276lb (125kg), but this was fitted in a turret of inclined rolled armour for enhanced protection, and the hull (based on that of the BT-7M) was also fitted with well-inclined armour as pioneered by the BT-IS to provide better ballistic protection against incoming projectiles. The crew was four (driver, bow machine-gunner, commander/gunner and loader), and the running gear was the standard Soviet wheel/track derivative of the Christie type, with four large-diameter road wheels (with torsion bar suspension) on each side.

The engine was a 450hp (336kW) V-2 diesel unit, which provided a maximum speed of 40.4mph (65km/h). This diesel was produced in prototype form during 1936, and marked a significant milestone in the development of tanks. Even in its early form the V-2 was powerful yet reliable, and offered the virtually priceless advantages of greater range on a given volume of fuel, the ability to run on easily produced diesel fuel, and lower volatility. This last fact was of particular interest to tank crews, who became all too aware during World War II of the alarming tendency of the fuel to ignite when a petrol-engined tank was hit,

Arguably the most important armoured fighting vehicle of World War II, the Soviet T-34 medium tank is seen here in one of its early forms with a 76.2mm (3in) main gun.

transforming a possibly survivable hit into an inferno from which few men were likely to emerge, and then only with serious burns.

The A-20 was evaluated against the T-III (otherwise T-46-5) prototype, which used a Christie-type suspension comprising six smaller-diameter road wheels on each side, together with three track-return rollers. The T-III was powered by a 300hp (224kW) diesel engine for a speed of 28mph (45km/h) at a weight of 62,832lb (28,500kg), and although armour thicknesses and armament were similar to those of the A-20, this latter was judged superior in all operational aspects largely as a result of its superior running gear and the better protection offered by its well-sloped armour. The only major criticism levelled at the A-20 was its modest armament, and this was improved in the A-30 that appeared at the beginning of 1939 by the adoption of a 76.2mm (3in) L/26.5 weapon. The A-30 was heavier than the A-20, and was hampered by a number of problems associated with the armament.

Koshkin had meanwhile moved forward to a revised concept, based on the revelation that Christie-suspended tanks spent virtually none of their time on their wheels rather than tracks. Koshkin was confirmed in his belief that the need for combined wheel and track capability was small (and added weight as well as mechanical complexity), and therefore moved forward to the development of the T-32, which was based on the A-20 and A-30 but without any provision for the tank to be stripped of its tracks so that it could run on its rubber-tyred road wheels. This allowed the use of wider tracks for reduced ground pressure and improved traction, and also permitted (with broadening of the hull) yet further sloped protection. The armour varied in thickness up to a maximum of 1.18in (30mm) on the hull and 1.77in (45mm) on the turret; other details were similar to those of the A-20 and A-30, with the notable exception of the running gear that now comprised five road wheels on each side. At a weight of 42,549lb (19,300kg) and with a standard crew of four, the T-32 could reach 37.3mph (60km/h).

Thus was the scene set for the T-34 (often called the T-34/76 in Western terminology for the calibre of its main gun), which appeared in prototype form at the end of 1939 for exhaustive evaluation and proving trials in the first half of 1940. Just after the beginning of these prototype trials, Koshkin succumbed to pneumonia and died, his place as chief designer being taken by Morozov and later by V.V. Krylov for the much-improved T-34/85 variant that appeared in 1943. The T-34/76 was a further development of the T-32 with a number of detail modifications and slightly thicker protection on the least protected areas for a weight of 58,918lb (26,725kg). The hull and turret were of welded construction, the latter fitted with an L/30.5 version of the 76.2mm (3in) gun, which fired its 13.78lb (6.25kg) shot with a muzzle velocity of 2,001ft (610m) per second. The T-34 was powered by a 500hp (373kW) diesel engine, which provided for a maximum speed of 32mph (51.5km/h), and the fuel capacity of 135 Imp gal (615 litres) offered the exceptional range of 280 miles (450km).

The hull was divided into three compartments. The forward compartment provided side-by-side seating for the driver and the bow machine-gunner (who doubled as radio operator in the company and platoon commanders' vehicles that were the only tanks fitted with this equipment). The fighting compartment was behind the short forward compartment rather than in the centre, and the engine compartment was at the rear. The transmission to the rear drive sprockets was also located in the rear compartment, and proved the least reliable single component of the T-34 (vehicles were often seen with a spare transmission unit lashed down on the rear decking). The running gear comprised five unequally spaced road wheels, each mounted on a trailing arm whose coil-spring suspension unit was located inside the hull: the two leading wheels had double concentric springs, and the other three had single springs.

The least successful tactical feature of the T-34/76 in its initial form was the turret, a small unit with manual or electric traverse through 360° and provision for manual geared elevation of the main armament through an arc between -3° and +30°. Mounted co-axially with the main armament was a 7.62mm (0.3in) DT machine-gun, and the bow machine-gun was a similar weapon. Ammunition stowage comprised 77 main-armament rounds (a mixed complement of armour-piercing, HE and shrapnel as required) and up to 3,000 machine-gun rounds, the latter in magazine form rather than belted form.

The T-34/76 entered production towards the middle of 1940 at factories located in Kharkov, Leningrad and Stalingrad, the first machines being delivered in June 1940. Germany's advance after the beginning of Unternehmen 'Barbarossa' immediately threatened the Kharkov and Leningrad production facilities, and these were part of the USSR's heavy industrial and war-making capability that was uprooted into the safety of Siberia: the Kharkov and Leningrad facilities were combined with the tractor factory at Chelyabinsk to create what became known as Tankograd, which is still one of the USSR's main centres for tank production. Exact production figures are uncertain, but the figures appear to be in the order of 115 machines in 1940, 2,800 in 1941, 5,000 in 1942, 10,000 in 1943, 11,750 in 1944 and 10,000 in 1945, giving a grand total of about 39,665 T-34s of all types.

The first production variant had the Western designation T-34/76A, and is the version described above with a welded turret carrying the Model 1939 L11 main gun. The welded turret was somewhat complex to build, and, as the Soviets possessed good capability for the production of large castings, a cast turret (still with the same L/30.5 gun in a rolled plate mounting) was introduced to allow turret production to match the steadily increasing tempo of hull production. During 1941 the Germans began to field an increasing number of 50mm PaK 38 anti-tank guns whose projectiles could pierce the T-34's armour at short ranges, and in response the Soviets increased the frontal armour of the T-34 to 1.85in (47mm) on the hull and 2.36in (60mm) on the turret; at much the same time, the original steel-tyred road wheels were supplanted by rubber-tyred wheels offering greater ride comfort for the crew.

In 1942 the Soviets introduced to the T-34 series the improved Model 1940 F34 gun with a longer barrel, a weapon that had been pioneered in the 1930s for the T-28 and T-35 tanks. This piece weighed 1,003lb (455kg) and had an overall length of 124.6in (3.165m), its L/41.2 barrel firing the same 13.78lb (6.25kg) shot as the Model 1939 gun, but with the higher muzzle velocity of 2,231ft (680m) per second for armour-penetration figures of 2.72in (69mm) at a range of 545yds (500m), 2.4in (61mm) at a range of 1,095yds (1,000m), 2.13in (54mm) at a range of 1,640yds (1,500m) and 1.89in (48mm) at a range of 2,185yds (2,000m). These figures compared favourably with the equivalents for the 75mm (2.95in) KwK L/24 and KwK 40 L/43 weapons carried by the Germans' contemporary PzKpfw IV tanks, but the T-34 scored decisively over its German adversaries in protection, range and cross-country performance. The use of the longer 76.2mm (3in) gun in the T-34 is signalled in Western terminology by the designation T-34/76B, and T-34/76Bs are associated with welded as well as cast turrets. Thicker armour and the cast turret increased the T-34/76B's weight to 62,831lb (28,500kg) without any serious degradation of performance.

Some criticism had been levelled at the provision of a single large forward-hinged hatch in the turret roof of these first models, and this deficiency was remedied in the T-34/76C that began to appear in 1943. This variant had twin hatches, increasing overall height from the 8ft 2in (2.49m) of the previous models to 8ft 10in (2.69m). Weight was boosted to 67,240lb (30,500kg), with a consequent decrease in maximum speed to 29.8mph (48km/h). Other features of the T-34/76C were spudded tracks, improved vision devices and an armoured sleeve for the bow machine-gun.

By the time the T-34/76C was beginning to enter service, the Soviets were well advanced with the development of the upgunned T-34/85 version, but saw considerable merit in maintaining the combat capability of the T-34/76 series with a number of improved features. The first of these was a revised hexagonal turret with a wider gun mounting/mantlet in a version known to the West as the T-34/76D: the new turret provided greater internal volume and, perhaps just as significantly, removed the earlier turrets' rear overhang, whose slight horizontal separation from the rear decking had given German assault pioneers an ideal spot for the placement of anti-tank mines. The new turret increased tank weight to 69,224lb (31,400kg), and another feature introduced on this variant, but then retrofitted without delay on earlier marks, was provision for jettisonable external fuel tanks to increase the T-34/76's already considerable range. The T-34/76E was basically similar, but had a welded turret complete with a commander's cupola. The final T-34/76F had a cast turret with the commander's cupola, and also introduced a five-speed gearbox; only very limited production was undertaken before the T-34/76 series was superseded by the T-34/85.

In autumn 1943 there appeared the T-34/85 with the new 85mm (3.35in) gun, designated initially as the D-5T85 or in upgraded form as the ZIS-S53; the gun was used with a turret adapted from that of the KV-85 heavy tank. The D-5T85 weighed 1,283lb (582kg) and possessed an overall length of 173.9in (4.42m): its L/51.5 barrel allowed the 20.635lb (9.36kg) armour-piercing shot to be fired with a muzzle velocity of 2,599ft (792m) per second, with APCBC, HE and HEAT rounds as alternatives. The ZIS-S53 weighed 2,531lb (1,148kg) and possessed an overall length of 173.9in (4.641m): its L/54.6 barrel allowed the 20.635lb (9.36kg) armour-piercing shot to be fired with a muzzle velocity of 2,625ft (800m) per second, thereby giving it sufficient kinetic energy to penetrate 4in (102mm) of armour at an angle of 0° at a range of 1,095yds (1,000m). With either of these weapons the T-34/85 was a devastating tank, completely outclassing the PzKpfw IV and providing a match for the Panther and Tiger in all but outright firepower at medium and long ranges. The main gun was provided with 55 rounds, and the secondary armament of two 7.62mm (0.3in) machine-guns (one bow and the other co-axial) had 2,394 rounds available to them. The larger turret had the considerable advantage of allowing a tactical crew of three, the availability of a gunner and loader permitting the commander to concentrate on his primary function.

The T-34/85 was authorised for production in December 1943, and by the year's end 283 had been built in convincing proof of the advantage of combining well-proved features (the hull of the T-34 with the turret/armament of the KV-85). By the end of 1944 some 11,000 T-34/85s had been delivered, and production continued into the post-war period: the type served with the Soviet armies until the mid-1950s, and it is still in moderately widespread use in many parts of the world.